Truth Be Told

LARRY KING

Truth Be Told

Off the Record about Favorite Guests,
Memorable Moments, Funniest Jokes,
and a Half Century of Asking Questions

WEINSTEIN
BOOKS

This book is dedicated to Hunter Waters.

Hunter was a *Larry King Live* producer who passed away with esophageal cancer early this year at the age of thirty-two.

I remain amazed by people of faith who can explain the passing of such a young, vital person. It always made me happy to see his smiling face. I always loved hearing the sound of his voice.

Rest well.

Contents

Truth Be Told

1

Time

I've never thought much about time, because I've always been too busy looking at my watch.

That sounds like something Yogi Berra might say. But it's true. You can't be a broadcaster without being extremely conscious of the clock. I'm never late. I remember a time after I had heart surgery. I was at the La Costa Resort, waiting for my surgeon to meet me so we could head to the airport. I said, "Jeez, where is he?" Somebody who knew him said, "He can be late. He's a surgeon. Surgery doesn't start without him."

A broadcaster cannot be late. Well, he can. But he'll be fired. For fifty-three years, my day has been planned around six o'clocks and nine o'clocks. It's hard to explain how conscious of the clock that makes you. I can only give you a sense.

Not only are you always conscious of the hour when you're in broadcasting, but you also have a heightened awareness of seconds. When you've repeatedly got to slide into a commercial break, you understand exactly how long five seconds lasts.

I used to have a cheap little clock on the set of *Larry King Live*. Every time Jerry Seinfeld came on as a guest he'd swipe it. It wasn't a case of: The show's over, here's your clock. He'd never give it back. I'd have to go to Radio Shack and buy another.

"Jerry," I finally said—after he took it for the third time. "Give the clock back."

"You don't need it," he said. "You've got a clock in your head."

He was right. But the strange thing about the clock in my head is that it always seems to be in the future. This is how it feels: Just say there's a miracle and I landed an interview with God on Monday night. It'd be on the front page of every newspaper: LARRY KING TO INTERVIEW GOD MONDAY. You know what I'd be thinking? *What am I going to be doing on Wednesday night?*

For fifty-three years, that's the way my mind has worked: thinking about what's next and constantly checking my watch to make sure I'm on time for it. But that's very different from stopping to *think* about time and the meaning of its passing.

As my CNN show wound down the last two weeks of its twenty-five-year run, a moment came that made me stop to reflect. During the final minute of a satellite interview with Vladimir Putin, the Russian prime minister invited me to Moscow. Then, through his interpreter, he turned the tables on me.

"Can I ask you one question?"

"Sure."

"In U.S. mass media," he said, "there are many talented and interesting people. But, still, there is just one king there. I don't ask why he is leaving. But, still, what do you think? We have a right to cry out: Long live the King! When will there be another man in the world as popular as you happen to be?"

I've never taken compliments well, and my head dipped. It's OK in broadcasting to look down at your notes for an instant. But your eyes can't become glued to your desk. My head just wouldn't come up. I doubt many broadcasters have been faced with a similar situation. It wasn't a mistake. A reaction isn't a mistake. I was humbled.

For the first time since May 1, 1957, I was speechless. That moment with Putin connected me to my first moment on the air.

As I lowered the music to my theme song in the control booth of a tiny radio station in Miami Beach, my mouth felt like cotton. I couldn't introduce myself. I opened my mouth, but no words came out. WAHR listeners must have wondered what the hell was going on when I took up the theme song again and lowered it once more. Again, no words came out. Maybe the audience could hear the pounding of my heart—but that was about it. I took up the theme song again, then brought it down for the third time. Nothing. That's when the station manager kicked open the control room door and screamed: "This is a communications business!"

It was as if he grabbed me by the shoulders and shook the words out of me. I told the microphone how all my life I'd dreamed of being a broadcaster. I told it how nervous I was. I told it how the station manager had just changed my name a few minutes earlier and then kicked open the door. I let myself be me, and the words started flowing.

So my career had started with an awkward moment of speechlessness. *I couldn't believe I was actually on the air.* And now my television show was approaching an end with another speechless moment. *The prime minister of Russia has just called me a king.*

The same lesson I learned on my first day guided me

through the awkwardness fifty-three years later: There's no trick to being yourself.

My head came up to look at Putin in the monitor. My words were not memorable, but they were sincere.

"Thank you. Thank you," I told him. "I have no answer to that."

In so many ways, the end has brought me back to the beginning. The moment with Putin makes me look back on everything that's happened since my mother came to America by boat from the tsar's Russia. I can picture my mother. If I close my eyes, I can even hear her voice: "*Again*, you're unemployed?"

She had a great sense of humor, Jenny Zeiger. The classic Jewish mother. Truth is, *only* my mother would have believed that a kid like me, who never went to college, could have had such success. The more I look back, the more unbelievable it becomes. There have been so many twists and turns.

I think of my earliest memories of the Russians. As a boy I rooted for them when I studied World War II maps in the newspapers. They were fighting the Germans on the second front. Everyone I knew loved Joe Stalin. Papa Joe, we called him.

By the time I got my first teenage kiss, we hated him. Stalin had seized the Eastern bloc.

There was panic in America the year I started in radio. *Sputnik* had been launched. We were no longer in the lead. The Soviets could look down on us. I was a married man with a young son when I saw tanks roll down the streets of Miami during the Cuban missile crisis.

Humor helps after moments like that. The comedian Mort Sahl did a funny bit on how things change: An American soldier gets knocked unconscious during World War II and doesn't wake up until more than fifteen years later.

"Get me my gun!" he says. "Get me my gun! I'm gonna go kill those Germans!"

"No, no," the doctors try to calm him, "the Germans are our friends."

"Are you crazy?" the soldier says, "We've got to help the Russians get the Germans."

"No, no, no. World War II ended years ago. The *Russians* are our enemies."

"I'll tell you what then," the soldier says. "Get me my gun so I can help the Chinese wipe out the Japs."

"No, no, no, no. The Japanese are now our friends. The Communist Chinese are our enemies."

"What a crazy world." The soldier shakes his head. "I'd better rest. I think I'll take a vacation. Maybe a couple of weeks in Cuba."

By the time the Vietnam War started, I was interviewing everyone from generals to Soviet defectors on local radio and television. I was Mr. Miami. We were told the war would stop the domino spread of Communism. Not long after we figured out our mistake, the Soviets made one of their own and invaded Afghanistan. By then, I was on all night, coast to coast. President Carter came on my Mutual Broadcasting radio show to explain the U.S. boycott of the Moscow Olympics.

I couldn't even get CNN on my television in Washington when Ted Turner started it. Ted didn't see the satellite as an enemy. One of the few rules he had when I joined CNN in 1985 was that we couldn't say the word *foreign*. Borders were crazy to him. He wanted to use satellites to bring people together.

By the time the Berlin Wall came down, the backdrop of my show was known around the world. Mikhail Gorbachev came to meet me for lunch wearing suspenders. Boris Yeltsin watched me announce that OJ was heading down the freeway in the white Bronco. When he arrived in the U.S. for a presidential conference, the first question Yeltsin whispered into President Clinton's ear was: "Did he do it?"

I think back to my mother and all those Jews who left the pogroms and Russia at the turn of the twentieth century. And I think of the irony of Putin telling me in our first meeting that his favorite place in the world to visit is Jerusalem.

How could it be that so much time has passed? Seems like I was just running down the streets of Bensonhurst with my friend Herbie to celebrate V-E Day. Suddenly, I'm celebrating my show's twenty-fifth anniversary? Then I'm announcing that my show is going to end? When I did, the most popular sports star in Washington, D.C., was the Russian hockey player Alexander Ovechkin. And Putin called to ask if he could make a final visit before I signed off. Maybe this is what Ted Turner had hoped for when he started the network.

Yes, we have come full circle. Once again, we can be friendly with the Russians. Everything changes, and everything stays the same. *Again*, you're unemployed?

Why is the world like this? I have no idea—only another good joke that confirms it.

A guy living in the Bronx takes his shoes in for repair. It's December 6, 1941. The next day, the Japanese bomb Pearl Harbor, and he enlists.

He goes overseas. He fights the war, meets a Japanese girl, marries her. He goes into business, lives in Tokyo for twenty-five years. One day he comes back to the United States for a business meeting. He's going through an old wallet and finds a ticket stub for that old pair of shoes. It's marked December 6, 1941.

He wonders if the shoe store is still there. So he asks his limo driver to take him up to the Bronx.

There it is! John's Shoe Repair.

"I'm gonna go in with the ticket," the guy tells the driver, "just to see what happens."

He walks in. It's the same repairman!

The guy hands John the repairman the ticket. John the repairman turns and shuffles to the back.

A minute later he returns to the counter and says, "They'll be ready next Tuesday."

2

Leaving

I'm not sure which comes first—acceptance or belief. When you first realize you're about to lose something that's a part of you, it's hard to accept. But even when you start to accept the loss, it's still hard to believe.

I knew my show had only a few months remaining when I sat down last September to interview the Iranian president Mahmoud Ahmadinejad for the third time. Yet as our final session ended, the words that left my mouth were: "We'll pick this up next year . . ."

You don't stop to think it's the last time you might be interviewing President George Bush 41 when he lifts himself out of a wheelchair to greet you. His leg was shaking from a variation of Parkinson's disease. He was eighty-six years old. What you do is talk about his plans to go skydiving.

Maybe my feelings about leaving can be traced back to my first memory of it—when my father left me. There was no warning. I was nine years old, walking home from the library carrying an armful of books. Three police cars were in front of my apartment. I started running up the steps when I heard my mother's screams. A cop came down the staircase straight for me. He picked me up and the books under my arm went flying. The cop put me in a police car and told me that my father had died of a heart attack.

I was bewildered at first. But then another emotion set in. I refused to cry. I didn't go to the funeral. I stayed home and bounced a spaldeen—the Spalding rubber ball we used to play stickball with—off the front stoop. Years later, when I mentioned to a psychologist how I had purposely recited prayers in synagogue in a way to provoke pity, he suggested that it might have been because I was angry—angry that my father had left me.

Of course, I now understand that it wasn't my father's fault. He certainly didn't want to leave me. But the day he left probably had more impact on my life than any other.

It may have seemed abrupt when I announced on my show in late June that I was leaving. But it was a process of evolution on my end. Looking back, there were several moments that foretold the change.

At the end of February, I got a call from my producer, Wendy Walker, and her top aide, Allison Marsh. They were elated. They'd just landed an interview with the head of the Toyota Motor Corporation, Akio Toyoda. There was no bigger story in the news at the time. Toyoda was testifying before Congress after the recent surge of accidents and deaths caused by unintended acceleration stemming from defective parts. "It'll be his only interview," Wendy said. "He doesn't want to be interviewed by anyone else."

I should have been happy. I'd been asking for a show on this topic for weeks. Not only were Wendy and the staff delivering—they were doing so big time. It doesn't get any better than booking the guy who runs the company. But there were a couple of catches. Akio Toyoda wanted to do the interview face-to-face. And since he was testifying in Washington, that meant I had to get on a plane in L.A. the following morning to get there on time.

CNN flies me private, so the plane was no problem. But there were personal issues. Not many people were aware, but I was fighting off prostate cancer at that point. I'd also had a stent placed in one of my arteries to open up a blockage. Doctors had advised me to take it easy and avoid stress. But that seemed almost impossible. I was going through a rough patch with my wife, and there was tension at home that we were trying to work out. Shawn has a history of migraine headaches and was not feeling well on the day Wendy's call came. I didn't want to leave her. Plus, I'd be flying off, coming right back, then flying to Washington again a few days later for my cardiac foundation fund-raiser. Something inside told me it was all too much.

"You can stay in Washington and do the show there until the fund-raiser," Wendy suggested. Wendy was going to take care of everything. But that would mean waiting around and being away from Shawn and my two young boys for a few days. I didn't want that, either.

"Akio Toyoda is going to be testifying before Congress all day," I told Wendy. "It's all going to be taped and he's going to be on every news channel. It's not like people aren't going to see him answering questions. I don't think I need to go."

Wendy must have been stunned. She'd been producing my show for seventeen years. I'd never turned down an interview of this magnitude before. Apart from my heart problems, I'd never called in sick. From the moment I got my first job as a deejay in Miami Beach, everyone at the station knew that if they needed to take a shift off, all they had to do was call Larry.

Larry would fill in. I could never get enough of the micro-phone. In my free time during those early days I had a second job announcing at the dog track. Then I took on a newspaper column and a local television show. On top of that, I'd speak for pleasure to audiences at the Rotary Club or Knights of Columbus. As the years passed, I took on even more. Back in the mid-'80s, I'd finish my CNN show in Washington, drive to Virginia to do my all-night talk-radio show on the Mutual net-work, get some sleep, then write a column for *USA Today* dur-ing the day—and then help raise money for my cardiac foundation to get heart operations for people who couldn't af-ford them. I was always prepared to work. Since the day I went on the air, I've never gotten drunk. I worked fifty-three straight days after 9/11. I often went to the studio to tape shows on Saturdays and Sundays. Shawn always wondered why we could never just get in a car and drive up the coast for a week. It seemed like a nice idea. I'd never say no. But we'd never make the trip. I guess the truth is that there was no micro-phone in the car. I think it was Woody Allen who said that 80 percent of life is showing up. Whenever CNN needed me, I was always there.

On top of that, I hardly ever say no to anyone. On one level, the absence of negativity is probably a reason why guests feel safe around me. That's why they're comfortable enough to open up. But never saying no can also be a huge fault. Ten people can ask me to do a favor at the same time on the same day, and I'll agree to all ten requests. I just don't want to let anybody down. Naturally, that's caused me to let down the people I didn't want to let down in the first place, and has got-ten me into trouble over the years. But I just don't have it in me to deny anyone anything. Fifty-year-old women I've never met approach me at breakfast with modeling portfolios and ask if

I can help them get a job in fashion. Yoga instructors show up with stretch mats and ask me to speak at their classes. Men with stashes of foreign bonds that for some reason they can't cash ask me if I know people who can help. *Why me?* I'm always asking as I step out after breakfast at Nate 'n Al's deli. But I know why. It's because I can't say no. That's why my friend Sid Young sits next to me at breakfast. He says no. Sid, and my lawyers.

Suddenly, *I'm saying no* to an interview that Barbara Walters and Oprah Winfrey would like to have? After my staff worked overtime to pull it off? At a time when the network's ratings were falling behind Fox and MSNBC, and negotiations were about to begin on my next contract?

I went to dinner with some friends that night but didn't feel like eating. After a while, I wanted to throw up. I left early, went home, but couldn't sleep. I tried to do a little reading, and finally dozed off. When I woke up it was just after midnight.

Yeah, I thought, Akio Toyoda is going to be testifying all day. Yeah, he's going to be all over the news. But I might get more out of him. A senator only cares about how the hearing affects American car owners. He has an agenda. I don't. I'd ask questions a senator wouldn't consider. "Your grandfather started the company. What do all these troubles mean for you when you are in front of your friends?" His answer to this question is going to be very different from the responses that everyone will see on clips from the hearing. There are interesting things that can come out of this interview, I thought, and the best way to get those answers is face-to-face.

I went to the bedroom and looked at Shawn. She was sleeping peacefully. She seemed to be feeling better. Now my mind was really starting to fly. I could take the kids to school. Then, if I flew out at ten in the morning, I'd get to Washington around five thirty in the afternoon. I could do the show, jump back on a plane to L.A. and be home by 1:30 a.m. That way I could take the boys to school the next morning.

What was I thinking? This is a piece of cake. I couldn't get back to sleep. So I called Wendy. It was 2:26 a.m.

"Hello! Wendy, it's Larry!"

"Larry . . ."

"Listen, if you can reach the Toyota people, tell them I'll do it."

We talked some more and then I got a few hours' sleep. When I awoke and opened the *New York Times* it said: Snow possible in Washington. I didn't care. I got some chewing gum for the flight. I was all set. Then I looked at my phone and saw a message to call Wendy.

The heart physician Dean Ornish had told her sometime before that I needed to avoid stress. She didn't want to put any more on me. She said she'd try to make the interview happen by satellite—and she did. It worked out well, got big play, and everybody was happy. But looking back, I realize: For the first time, I'd said no.

The tension in my marriage kept building. I'll get into this later on. I definitely want to clear up some misconceptions. But for now, I want to focus on how I came to leave my show and the ups and downs that came with it. So I'll stick to the basics.

On the morning after opening day at Dodger Stadium, we got into a loud argument outside the house. I had made a mistake, and Shawn found out about it. The mistake—whether big or small—is nobody's business. It's between Shawn and me. I just wanted to move past it and get on with our lives. That's how I deal with mistakes. My friend Sid was with me. I got so upset that I just wanted to get away. We weren't exactly in Tiger Woods territory, but in driving off I nearly ran over Sid's toe.

It's impossible to know how Shawn felt. I felt like I was

going to have a heart attack. We both filed for divorce. But there was no sense of relief. It was a miserable day. I was exhausted and didn't know how I could do the show. Willie Nelson was the scheduled guest. He has a great line about divorce: "It costs so much because it's worth it." But it wasn't amusing that day. I felt hollow as I went to the studio. Then the lights came on. It always amazes me what happens when the camera starts rolling. No matter how low or tired I feel, I shoot right up. I have no idea where this energy comes from. But there's nothing in the world like it. Willie and I had a great hour. We sang "Blue Skies." Shawn had recorded with Willie, and—shows you where my mind was—we talked about the two of them singing together in the future as if the divorce filings had never happened.

That night was one of the worst of my life.

I was in a hotel room only a couple of miles away from my home but it felt like I'd abandoned my sons. Chance had just turned eleven. Cannon was nine—the same age I was when my father died. Garth Brooks says that every curse is a blessing and every blessing's a curse. That night, I think both Shawn and I understood exactly what he meant. It was a sleepless night that didn't seem to end. But I think it made us both realize that we didn't want to leave our kids. We didn't want to leave our home. And we didn't want to leave each other. I just wanted the funny, smart, and beautiful woman I married twelve years before to reappear and the arguments to stop.

Millions of couples in America have gone through the same process and emotions. But getting things back together is not easy when you're on worldwide television and you've been married seven times before to six other women. That last fact alone gives late-night comics an irresistible punch line. Look, I'm not going to deny that I've made some mistakes along the way. But

Shawn and I had been married for twelve years. That ain't small potatoes. I have a good family. Somehow facts like that get lost when a celebrity marriage has trouble. The simplest act—like coming together to watch our sons play a Little League baseball game—became surreal. One night shortly after the divorce filing, there were at least sixty paparazzi snapping away at my bewildered kids as we tried to walk through the darkness to our cars. Shawn's mother got knocked over. Cannon started crying. Shawn put Cannon on her back to protect him, threw a jacket over his head and ran down a hill with cameras flashing all around them. If I had known this was going to happen, would I ever have entered the lawyer's office?

It took us a while to rescind the divorce papers and work things out. In the meantime, a bad vibe circulated. There's a line between mean and funny. It felt like many of the late-night jokes crossed to the wrong side. The tabloids and Internet sites had a field day. The problem with the tabloid attention was that it set another dynamic in motion. The mainstream press started to examine CNN's declining ratings. I was a symbol for the network, and the writers were beginning to wonder if time had begun to pass me by. It's only natural for your staff to fight back to improve the ratings. The easiest way to do that is to book tabloid-style stories. If I disliked tabloid shows in the first place, imagine how I felt doing them when my own marriage had become one. The situation might have continued spiraling downhill if not for one saving grace: The twenty-fifth anniversary of my show was approaching.

President Obama, Lady Gaga, LeBron James, and Bill Gates were lined up as guests back to back. Another show was assembled to look at the best moments over a quarter century. It was an amazing week, and it changed the energy and the conversation. Flying back home from the White

House I was on a high. That's when everything seemed to
come into focus.

In a single week, I'd sat down with the president of the
United States, the hottest stars in music and sports, and a billionaire who was changing the world through philanthropy.
Was it ever going to get any better that that? Or was I looking
at a future of shows with fifteen reporters and analysts who'd
never met Sandra Bullock all talking about her marital problems in order to prop up the ratings?

It was a year before my contract was up—the time we tra-
ditionally start working out a new one. I sometimes wonder
what would have happened if Ted Turner were still running the
network. Ted hired me in less than twenty-four hours, and I'm
sure the meeting would have been completely different. He's an
extremely loyal guy and he would have figured out some way—
any way—to keep me in front of the microphone. Negotiations
were always swift and ended in three-, four-, or five-year contracts. But the Ted Turner who hired me back in 1985 had the
only cable news game around. The network's execs twenty-five
years later—Jim Walton, Phil Kent, and Jon Klein—were competing in a different world.

If I had to compare myself to a ballplayer as I entered the
meeting, I'd identify myself with the New York Yankees short-
stop Derek Jeter. I was getting older. I hadn't had my best year.
But there were some high moments. I was associated with the
network the way Jeter is with Yankee pinstripes. The backdrop
to my show is one of the most recognizable images in the world.
Attendance might have been down, but CNN was making a nice
profit—just like the Yanks. And some of the reasons for the de-
cline in my show's ratings were not my own. The show leading
in to mine was having a difficult time and the host ended up
leaving in the middle of the year. It's no different from baseball:

If the player batting before you is hitting .350, you're going to see better pitches and have a higher average. I didn't have the benefit of a large audience rolling into my show. This may be a stretch, but to continue the analogy, CNN was asking me to sacrifice my numbers by moving a base runner along. Joy Behar started out as a guest on my show, then guest hosted. She's funny, got a great spirit, and she was given her own show on *CNN Headline News* in my time slot, nine o'clock. I get it. The idea is to bring in as many viewers as possible and make the most money for the network. That's corporate America. The guys at Pontiac try to beat the brains out of the guys from Buick even though they both work for General Motors. Believe me, nobody was happier than me to see Joy's mounting success. But fair is fair. I'm sure that on some nights viewers were curious about Joy and her guests and clicked the remote to her show. My own network was cutting into my ratings and then wondering why they were falling.

The bottom line is, just as I'm sure Jeter wants to play for as long as he can with the Yankees, I wanted to stay with CNN. Over and over, the execs had told me, "You're here as long as you like." I figured I would be. My thoughts going into the meeting were simple. Maybe we can just lighten the workload a little and tone down the tabloid stuff.

The execs at CNN are very much in the position of baseball executives. They have to compete on the field and simultaneously prepare for the future. If they don't, they fail. Fail, and they get fired. So they have to protect themselves in a way that Ted Turner didn't. Ted was the owner. Ted cared more about money than ratings. If you said to Ted, which do you prefer, to be first in the ratings and make 1 million or be third in the ratings and make $1.3 million? He'd say, give me the $1.3 million. CNN was doing very well. It was making more money than Fox. But it was easy to see management's point of view. Broadcasting is not the same as it was in 1993 when 16 million people tuned in to the debate on my show between Vice President Al Gore and Ross Perot. The market has been fractured and tastes have changed. People are tuning in to cable news now not so much to get educated as to be entertained and have their own political opinions reinforced. A host like Bill O'Reilly uses his guests as props. One of the Nate 'n Al's breakfast gang once said that if Glenn Beck could get Kleenex as a sponsor he'd weep on cue four times a day. CNN's execs were competing in that world—and their prime-time guy was about to turn seventy-seven. Their prime-time guy would never beat down his guests. Their prime-time guy didn't want to do the tabloid stuff.

They made their proposal. It was not for the multi-year contract I was expecting. Maybe I felt something that every player who's been on the all-star team feels when the days of the long-term contracts end. Whatever happened to "You're here as long as you like"? Maybe broadcasting had changed, but there were still a lot of people who wanted to see me do what I do. I know this because I hear from them every day. They prefer to see people they're curious about candidly talking about their lives. They aren't interested in the shock and gossip tabloid stuff. But hey, the bottom line is, if the host ain't happy, we're all just spinning our wheels.

There was some back-and-forth between CNN, my agency, and my lawyer, Bert Fields. Bert came to me and said, How about this? You'll work a few more months until they get a replacement. You'll be paid the full final year of your contract. And then, for three years after that, you do a series of four specials a year on mutually agreeable subjects.

The specials would be for less money than I was making at the time, but it was still good money, and I'd be a free man.

I could work for other networks. I could do commercials. I could do the one-man comedy show onstage that I'd always wanted to do. I would no longer have to clear anything with CNN. Their only condition was that during the period of the agreement I couldn't work for MSNBC or Fox.

It sounded good. I'd be able to spend more time with Shawn and the kids, I'd still be with CNN, plus I could do things on my bucket list. At the same time, it sounded sad. Not only would I be leaving the show, but forty people I really cared about would be losing their jobs.

I thought it over. It felt like the right way to go. Wendy got a hold of the comedian Bill Maher. He moved an engagement so he could be my guest the night I announced my decision to leave. The toughest part was saying goodbye to the staff. They were losing their jobs and they were crying *for me*. It was good to have Bill as a guest. Humor always helps.

Soon after he heard the news, Colin Powell called to wish me well. He passed on a piece of advice that had been passed on to him by a brigadier general: "When the subway gets to the last stop and is getting ready to go back, it's time to get off the train." He said I got off at the right time.

The calls and good wishes from so many friends were incredibly uplifting. For months the press had been wondering: Has time passed him by? Now the response was: *Oh, no! What are we losing?* But it felt awkward when people started to congratulate me on my retirement. Retirement? Who said I was retiring? Retiring to what? I started to wonder what I was going to do when the show did end. I'm a creature of routine. What happens when there's no Wednesday night? There has to be a Wednesday night, because I'm a productive fellow. Thinking about no Wednesday night started to make me depressed. A psychologist told me that I was sitting shiva for my show. Shiva is the traditional ritual in Judaism used to comfort relatives of the deceased. The show was not dead yet. But it felt like the family was gathering.

A few weeks after the announcement, something happened that I'd never seen before. A free-agent basketball star got a one-hour prime-time special on ESPN to announce whether he would stay with his team or leave for another city. I wasn't able to watch LeBron James's decision live. My own show was on up against it. But I did get to see it on tape. It was a lesson in how not to leave.

I was surprised because of what I'd seen in LeBron a few weeks before when I spent the day at his home in Akron. I found him to be humble, very bright, and a good conversationalist. There was a moment that really stood out. We were walking to the basketball court he has outside his house to shoot some hoops when he told his son, "*Larry King* is in my house. If you would have told me that Larry King would be in my house when I was a kid, I never would have believed it." He wasn't buttering me up. He said it after the interview—not before. It was sincere and respectful. Which was the opposite of the way he came off when he announced his decision on live television.

LeBron grew up about half an hour away from Cleveland. He'd played his first seven years in the NBA for the Cavaliers. He'd carried the team on his back to the NBA finals. Cleveland hadn't won a championship in any sport since 1964, and he was seen as a savior. LeBron was beloved in Cleveland and celebrated almost everywhere else. Nobody could hate LeBron James. If you paid good money to see your team play against LeBron, and he beat you with a last-second shot, you weren't mad. You were grateful that you were in the arena that night to see him make that shot.

Then he went on the air and said, "I'm taking my talents to South Beach." He wasn't even going to be playing in South Beach. He was going to play in Miami—on the other side of the bay. By saying those two words, *South Beach*, he implied *girls*, bathing suits, hip. Everything that isn't Cleveland. So it came off as a put-down. The broadcast had been arranged by LeBron to raise money for the Boys and Girls Clubs of America. But by the end, the world saw people in Cleveland burning his jersey.

It was the first topic of conversation at the breakfast table at Nate 'n Al's the next morning. Nobody denied LeBron had every right to move. He was a free agent, and he shouldn't be told where he had to work. Ask any basketball player where he'd rather be in January—Cleveland or Miami—and it's not hard to guess the answer. Given the emotional ties, you'd have to call LeBron's decision courageous in many ways. But the way LeBron left made you wonder if he should have stayed. It also made me wonder how people leave, and how I would when the time came.

When Walter Cronkite came on my show at the age of eighty-six, he was wearing his CBS cuff links. But he was not happy when the network made him give up his anchor spot because of a rule that enforced retirement at sixty-five.

Dan Rather left CBS in anger after forty-four years of service. This after his reportage on a story about George Bush 43's Air National Guard service was attacked. The president of CBS told me that everything Dan reported was true, he just didn't have original documents. Dan got a bum rap, and he filed a $70 million lawsuit against the network that was thrown out of court. I'm sure that's not the way he wanted to go.

George Bush 43 has had a classy and gracious departure.

He's been uncritical of the current administration and he wrote a pretty good book. He was honest enough to admit that when he made his decision to invade Iraq, it was more instinctive than intellectual: *Damnit, I'm going to go.* His approval ratings are higher now than when he was president.

Bill Clinton hated to leave the White House. During Bush's inauguration, Clinton was hanging around the podium. He just did not want to leave. The honesty in that makes me smile.

I remembered Harry Truman walking to the train station after Eisenhower was inaugurated. There was no Secret Service protection for former presidents at the time. Truman just said goodbye and got on a train like a guy who had finished a day's work and was going home. That's dignity.

Sometimes the end can be confusing. There's a story about the comedian Milton Berle getting called up to take a stage bow at a late age. He could barely walk to the stage. But as soon as he did, he started telling jokes. He did four minutes—had the crowd going wild. My friend George Schlatter was watching and he called Berle the next morning. "Ruth," he said, when Berle's wife picked up the phone, "last night Milton was just wonderful."

Ruth said, "He came home and was just sick about it."

"Why?"

"He could only remember four minutes of material and he had to get off."

Berle thought he'd bombed because he couldn't go any longer.

Maybe leaving is hardest on athletes, because they seem to get old so much sooner than the rest of us. Why did Willie Mays have to stay that extra year? Nobody wants to see Willie Mays drop a fly ball. I have great respect for Jim Brown and Sandy

Koufax. Jim was maybe the best running back ever in profes-
sional football. He left at the height of his career on his own
terms to make movies—and he became a star. Boy, did Koufax
do it with style and grace. He had arthritis in the elbow. The
doctor said, We could treat you, and you could pitch. But any
one pitch might leave you with no use of your left arm. That
wasn't worth it to Sandy. He never had the surgery, he simply
left, but he still throws batting practice at spring training.

I remember when Michael Jordan left. I was one of the em-
cees on the night his statue was unveiled in front of the Bulls'
arena. Michael had conquered everything that had been set in
front of him in basketball and was leaving to see if he could suc-
ceed at baseball. All great athletes, Tommy Lasorda says, have
enormous faith in themselves. But not many would try to switch
sports at the height of their career. It was cold that night, and
we had to wait until the crew threw it to us from inside the
arena. While the two of us were standing by that statue, Michael
said, "I hope I can hit." That was a gutsy decision.

Maybe the best farewell ever was Lou Gehrig's at Yankee
Stadium. The whole thing must have been bewildering to him,
because it was inexplicable to everyone else. He was a hulky
guy and all of a sudden, he started to lose it. My cousin Bernie
told me he'd swing and you'd expect the ball to fly out of the
park but it would only be a pop-up. Nobody knew anything
about his disease before he got it. That's why it became known
as Lou Gehrig's disease. I was eight years old and didn't hear
his famous speech. Most people remember the speech scene
from the movie about him starring Gary Cooper. But when you
go back and listen to the actual speech in its entirety, it's surprising. It's much longer than you think. Gehrig was rather shy
and not known as an eloquent man. But he spoke quite a bit
about the disease, about his teammates, about hearing from

the hated New York Giants. He was eloquent when it counted. Given his situation, his words are about as good an exit as you can make: "I consider myself the luckiest man alive."

Then I thought of the worst way to go. Oddly enough, the guy who came to mind was a guy I once replaced—Walter Winchell.

Never again in the history of the media will anyone be what Winchell was. Young people don't know him, but there's never been a more powerful journalist. He had a radio show every Sunday night that all of America listened to. He also wrote a gossip column that was syndicated in about five hundred newspapers. In New York, everybody would buy the *Mirror* and turn to his column on page eleven. He must have had eight million readers a day. He invented words. If a famous couple was going to have a baby, they were *infantesimizing*. He discovered stars. He hurt them. Ninety-nine percent of what he reported was true— because anyone who tipped him wrong about a celebrity divorce never got in his column again. He used to ride with police squad cars at night to get stories. Louis Lepke, the gangster who ran the Italian mob's hit squad, Murder Incorporated, turned himself in to Winchell. He was afraid he would be shot in the street. Through a source, he said, "I will surrender only to Winchell." And it was Winchell who brought him in. Franklin Roosevelt courted Winchell, gave him entrée to the White House. Roosevelt realized Winchell's power and used it. So did FBI chief J. Edgar Hoover. Winchell became so big they made a special law to stop him from tipping stocks.

What started to derail Winchell was an incident involving Josephine Baker, the black singer and performer. She went to the Stork Club with some friends, got a seat, but the waiters wouldn't serve her. She'd call after them, and they'd keep walking by. She got mad, and news of the incident hit the press. Everybody started to rap the Stork Club. One of Winchell's friends owned the Stork Club, and Winchell came to his defense. In doing so, he labeled Baker a Communist.

That started his descent. Frank Sinatra announced that he would go to the Stork Club only if Abraham Lincoln made the reservation. When Roosevelt died and Truman became President, Winchell's access to the White House ended.

Papers started to drop him. I was the guy who replaced him at the *Miami Herald*. Down, down, down, he went. It couldn't get sadder. Toward the end, he'd type a column, mimeograph it, and hand it out on street corners.

We began to think of guests for my last shows. So many wonderful and accomplished people were considered for the last two weeks. Many accepted. Some were unavailable. In the end, the lineup worked out almost perfectly because the guests reflected nearly all the subjects that had been discussed on the show during the past twenty-five years. World events. Politics. Film. Crime. Music. Money. Medicine. Technology. The media. In fact, the show's final two weeks made the perfect table of contents for this book. Each day seemed like another chapter.

But when it came time to think about the final guest, there was one name that immediately came to mind: Mario Cuomo. The former governor of New York was the best speaker of our time and a good friend of mine. He came to the hospital when I had heart surgery. He invited me to spend a night at the Governor's Mansion. He and his wife danced in a conga line at my seventieth birthday party at Sammy's Romanian restaurant on the Lower East Side. So we called him. We said: December 16 is our last night. You were the first guest, you be the last. We'll fly you out. Mario accepted.

But then on his show, which led into mine, Eliot Spitzer said something uncomplimentary about Cuomo's son, Andrew. Andrew was running for governor of New York. Even though Spitzer followed up by giving Andrew his endorsement, Mario never forgave. He canceled. Maybe in his mind he was thinking, *This is familia. Hit my family, and you hit me.* It must be like *The Godfather.*

But why hold it against me? I didn't do anything. *Let me work this out*, I thought. I called him. I knew that if I could get him on the phone, I had him. But he didn't take the call. I left him a long message. Nothing. We tried Andrew. Nothing again.

It was perplexing. Morning after morning I left breakfast at Nate 'n Al's wondering: Why?

And that's the thing: *There were still unanswered questions.*

I remembered an interviewer at a radio station who quit and shifted to management. When I asked him why, he said, "I've asked every question and heard every answer." Not me. After fifty-three years, I'm still not out of questions. Either events bring them up or they just keep popping into my head.

Why do people close their eyes when they sneeze?

Do we still make razor blades in America?

Why don't you laugh when you tickle yourself?

Which made me wonder: What was I going to do with all my questions when I no longer had a show to ask them on?

3

Riches

The day after the Putin interview aired was one of the best of my life: The richest man in the world came on my show and then over to my house for a dinner party. Where I came from in Brooklyn, we didn't have dinner parties. Your aunts and uncles came over for *supper.*

After my father died, my family went on welfare—only in those days it wasn't called welfare. It was called Relief. I can remember an inspector coming over to look in our refrigerator. My mother was only supposed to buy choice meat, not top Grade A. But she bought top Grade A so her children could have the best and took less for herself. Those are the things you don't forget. And now I was hosting a dinner party for the richest guy in the world.

It's only natural to think of money when you hear the name Carlos Slim. Just before I interviewed him, his personal wealth was estimated at almost $54 billion. It was said that he was allergic to interviews, so nobody really knew much about him. To the public, he was not so much a man as he was a gigantic number that you saw in *Forbes* magazine.

Someone in our breakfast gang at Nate 'n Al's couldn't help but wonder about the interest on $54 billion at 5 percent and started calculating.

"That's $2.7 billion a year."

"Fifty-two weeks into that is how much?"

"About $52 million a week."

"Seven days in a week . . ."

"Comes to more than $7 million a day."

It's wild to think about it. If Carlos Slim decided to retire and do nothing, the *interest* on his money would be more than seven million *a day*.

Carlos owns the Mexican phone system and the largest grocery store chain in Central America. In 1997, he bought 7 percent of Apple. I can remember a conversation I had with the media mogul Haim Saban about Carlos. Haim is a billionaire several times over too. He runs Univision, the largest Spanish-speaking network in America. "There *is* such a thing as a billionaire's club," Haim said. "We all talk the same language. But every time I hear Carlos Slim's name I feel like a pauper."

It's only natural for me to be curious about men of great wealth, because money has always been something of a mystery to me. I remember a time when I was a kid when my friend Herbie asked, If you could make $100 a day, how many days a week would you work? I said, "Two. If I could make ten thousand dollars a year for the rest of my life . . . I'll take that deal. Where do I sign?" That was twice what my father ever made.

I'm certainly aware of the fascination many people have with money. But to this day, money has never really meant that much to me. All I ever really wanted to do was talk into a microphone. Somehow, money came with it. Not only that, but access to people who'd accumulated fortunes. I've always been more fascinated by the singer than the song. So my curiosity lies in the billionaire—not the billions.

I've interviewed many men of great wealth. It's always intriguing to see how they all came to their riches—because one thing that always struck me was how different their circumstances were.

Carlos Slim's father started their empire with a dry goods store and died when Carlos was thirteen—leaving behind $20 million that Carlos would turn into billions. Steve Wynn's father died just as Steve graduated from college—leaving behind substantial debt. Warren Buffett's dad was a congressman. Ted Turner's father committed suicide.

Kirk Kerkorian and Donald Trump both own hotels. Kirk turned thirteen in the Depression, never went past eighth grade and started out installing water heaters. He is intensely private and would never do an interview. Donald went to the Wharton business school at U. Penn. He puts his last name on everything he owns, and I interviewed him on my show at least twenty times. Art Linkletter was known to everyone in America as a television-show host and interviewer of kids. Few realized that he was an entrepreneur who introduced the motel to Australia, once owned a piece of the photo concessions at Disneyland, and financed the Hula Hoop.

They're all so different, yet the same basic qualities seem to run through them. They wonder about things. They're very strong in their convictions even though they're open to the other side. They're loyal. They have a love of numbers. They're risk takers. And they keep at it, even when the safest move would be to cash out and go home. As the comedian Albert Brooks says: You can sell off everything and move to an island. But the mind of a billionaire wouldn't do that.

These are qualities you'd like in your friends. So it's no wonder I've become close with many of them. When you get to know them, you find that money to them is simply a by-product of what they do.

Take Donald Trump. He's in real estate. Real estate is all about cultivating relationships and getting an edge. That's what he's great at. There was a well-known moment on the show when I asked him how he gets the edge. He casually continued the conversation and then, out of nowhere, said: "Do you mind if I sit back a little bit? Because your breath is very bad. Has this ever been told to you before?"

He threw me for a moment . . . and a lot of viewers for longer than that moment. We all thought he was being serious. He took a lot of heat the next day. *How could you do that to Larry?* They didn't understand it had nothing to do with my breath. My breath was perfectly fine. Donald was just making a point. He was showing how someone could be put off guard. The concept is: Perception is reality. Which is what Trump is all about. Donald has almost become a caricature of himself. But it works because he uses it to his advantage. The money comes because of his talent and passion for getting that edge. Take it from me—I'm living proof. As soon as I left my show last December, I was free to make endorsements. One of the first companies to seek me out makes breath mints. Thanks to Donald Trump, I am now an official spokesman for BreathGemz.

Steve Wynn's talent is an ability to see the world the way nobody else can. This is ironic because he has an eye disease called retinitis pigmentosa, which gives him tunnel vision. Not only can Steve imagine resorts that have never been conceived, but he has a way of looking inside people and figuring out how to get what he wants by giving them what they want. He could be a master psychologist.

A prime example is how he brought Garth Brooks to the Encore in Las Vegas. Garth was happily retired—he didn't need money, and he didn't want to be away from his family. He was simply looking for someone with influence to help out his charity. At the same time, Steve was looking for an act to fill the theater at the Encore because Danny Gans had suddenly passed away. A meeting was set between the two.

Garth had a plan to get Steve to donate a lot of money to his charity, but also to let him down easy and tell him he wasn't going to come out of retirement. In the end, Garth jokes, Steve didn't give him a single dollar for the charity, and Garth ended up working for Steve. The show happened because Steve realized that Garth loved to perform, but had retired simply to be with his family. So Steve got Garth a private plane that could fly him back and forth from Oklahoma. There's a two-hour time difference between Garth's home and the Encore—and it's a two-hour flight. Garth could leave at six thirty after his daughters' soccer game and arrive in Las Vegas at six thirty—an hour before curtain. He didn't even need to get made up, he could just walk out onstage in his street clothes and play. No band, just pure Garth and the music that made him who he'd become. Steve gave his audience a show that nobody had ever seen. And he gave Garth the chance to do what he loved and be home with his daughters a few hours after the concert.

When you can master the win-win, you inspire loyalty. Few are better at it than Ted Turner and Kirk Kerkorian. People who work for Kirk love him. Kirk knows everything that's going on, but he doesn't smother his employees. He gives them room to grow and moves them up. A lot of his managers used to be clerks.

I've never felt a greater loyalty to anyone I've ever worked with than Ted. Once, in the late eighties, when my contract was coming up, rival companies offered deals that doubled my salary. Ted was expanding at the time and couldn't counter with that kind of money. So my agent went to his office to tell him I was leaving. Ted picked up the phone, called me in the early morning at my hotel in California and said, "Here's what I want you to do. It's simple. Just say: 'Goodbye, Ted.' You say, 'Goodbye, Ted,' and we're friends. You start your new job and nobody's angry. I want to hear you say goodbye."

I stood in the suite in my underwear with the telephone at my ear. I just couldn't say "Goodbye, Ted."

"You can't say it!" Ted said. "You can't say it!" Then he promised me that within a year I'd have a contract for the same money I'd been offered—and he delivered.

Even when it looks like these guys are going to lose they find a way to win. Like when Ted and Kirk dealt with each other. Ted loved the movie *Gone with the Wind*. It led him to buy the studio that owned it—MGM—from Kirk for $1.5 billion. Just driving into the studio made Ted happy. But after a short time he found out that he really didn't like a business where you invest $42 million in a project and then at two o'clock on Monday morning find out whether you've made money or not. So he called Kirk and told him he'd like to sell it back at a loss. Who wouldn't want that deal? Sure, Kirk said, I'll buy it back at a profit.

Just one thing, Ted said. He wanted to keep the library. This was back in the mid-eighties. At the time, there was little to be done with the library. Plus, Kirk wasn't in television or cable. But Ted was. He knew exactly what to do with the library: Turner Classic Movies. So it was a win-win all around. Ted buys it, sells it back to Kirk at a loss, but keeps the movies and makes an enormous profit.

On the surface, the one quality these men have that I don't

is the passion to acquire. I don't amass companies or properties. But in a way, I guess you could say I do acquire. I acquire people. The joy of my life is meeting somebody interesting every day.

And at seventy-seven, I was getting to interview the richest guy in the world.

I had first met Carlos only a few months before. Carlos gives twelve thousand scholarships to Mexican kids every year and he invited me to speak to them at an annual event in Mexico City. Bill Clinton had spoken at the event, as had Colin Powell and Madeleine Albright. The director of *Avatar*, James Cameron, and I were invited in 2010. So was the former United Nations secretary general Kofi Annan.

A few days before the event, once again I felt I should be spending more time with my kids and I sent word that I was sorry but it was best for me to cancel. It was almost like fate called back and said, *You don't understand.*

I'm so glad I reconsidered. Saying no would have been the second biggest mistake of my life. The biggest will always be starting to smoke cigarettes when I was seventeen. It took me thirty-seven years to stop.

The night before the event, I had dinner with Carlos's assistant and learned that Carlos and I shared the same passion. As soon as we met, before we even said hello, we were talking baseball.

He's a crazy Yankee fan. He's seventy years old, and he knew about all the black major leaguers who'd come to play in the Mexican Leagues during the days of segregation. It wasn't long before we were arguing about the five greatest pitchers of all time.

How can you leave out Koufax?

But you had to take everything he said seriously. He knew his stats. He later showed me a two-page letter he'd hand-written to Alex Rodriguez. He listed all the things A-Rod needed to do, and the time he needed to do them in, in order to top numerous records. It was an amazing array of statistics.

I couldn't help but wonder: How could a guy with that kind of passion and those kinds of means not own a team? Divorce had recently left the Dodgers ownership in disarray, and so I just came out and asked, "Why don't you buy the Dodgers?"

His answer tells you a lot about him as a businessman. "You own a baseball team and you marry the team," he said. "It emotionally affects you. Did they win today? Did they lose today? You never want to be married to something you own."

I knew I was at the scholarship event simply to speak. But I couldn't help it. This is a guy, I thought, that I'd love to interview.

I never know what I'm going to say before I start to speak. I'm always living in the moment. I was told to tell a few stories and then we'd do some questions and answers. But when I reached the stage, I thought, Jeez, what am I going to say to these kids? I didn't know how many understood English. My stories are all built around humor, and they might not work so well if the timing got lost in translation. I took another look at the kids. It just felt right to tell the Moppo story. I figured they'd like it because it takes place in the last year of junior high school. I didn't realize at the time that something deeper was at work.

The Moppo story takes about fifteen minutes, start to finish. If you listened to my all-night radio show years ago you've probably heard it. And if you haven't heard it, make sure you get a ticket when my comedy show goes on the road. It's about a kid in our neighborhood named Gil Mermelstein, who got his nickname because he had a mop of hair. This is the setup: Moppo comes down with tuberculosis and to recover, moves to Arizona with his family on short notice. Nobody in the neighborhood knows. The only reason I found out was I was walking past his apartment with a couple of friends when we ran into one of Moppo's cousins. The cousin had been sent to tell the school that Moppo would be gone for the year. My best friend, Herbie, tells the cousin not to bother. *We'll* tell the school, he says. That's because Herbie's got a great idea, a surefire way for us to get up some money for hot dogs at Coney Island. Herbie wants to tell everyone at school that Moppo has died. That way, we can take up a collection for flowers for Moppo's family—and use the money to get the hot dogs. It's foolproof. Moppo's family is in Arizona, and the phone line in their apartment has been disconnected. Nobody would discover what we'd done until Moppo returned the next year—and by then we'd have all moved on to high school.

Our plan worked perfectly. Too perfectly. The principal found out about our flower collection and became so moved that he organized an end-of-the-year assembly in honor of the late Gil Mermelstein. At this assembly, an award was going to be presented to a high-achieving student. Not only that, but he asked me, Herbie, and Brazzi Abbate, our third conspirator, to be onstage when the award was presented. And! The principal invited the *New York Times* to cover the event.

You can imagine what happened when Moppo made one of the great recoveries in medical history and returned to school on the very day and hour of the assembly.

The translator was spontaneous and brilliant. The kids cracked up at all the right points. They had so many questions afterward. My part of the presentation started to go longer than the allotted time and someone put up a signal to stop, but Carlos Slim just waved his hand as if to say "Let it go."

His assistant had made plans to take me on a tour of Mexico City and show me some of the family's artwork. I later found out that when Carlos heard, he said, "No, no. *I'm* taking Larry. Get me a car."

It's not often that Carlos drives—for reasons of security. But you never would have known. He was weaving through the streets, showing me where he played when he was a kid. What a vibrant place. Such beautiful architecture—I had no idea. It made me realize how much time I've spent in the studio in front of a backdrop of the world, yet there is so much of that world I haven't seen. But it's never been about touring the pyramids for me. It's always been about the people I meet. The great part of the ride was the feeling. Carlos was showing me around the old neighborhood like a guy from Brooklyn.

Garth Brooks says that there are people who you hear are extraordinary, and then you meet them and find out they're ordinary—and that's what makes them extraordinary. That's the definition of Carlos Slim. I'd never met a guy quite like him—and yet meeting him felt like the first day I met my oldest pal, Herbie.

My temporary cancellation never came up in our conversation. But if we'd talked about it, I think Carlos would have understood. I wanted to spend the time with my boys, and everything about Carlos revolves around family. He has three sons and three daughters. The sons all grew up in one room. The daughters grew up in another. Carlos obviously could afford to give them each their own room. The point was, he wanted them to be close. One brother gave another a kidney.

Carlos's wife died of kidney disease. He moved to a much

more modest home, but he kept the old house exactly the way it was. He won't even reupholster a chair. He is as attached to that house as I am to the stories of my childhood. His wife had turned him on to art, and he had accumulated some incredible pieces. He's got Dalí's *Christ of Saint John of the Cross*. You know that Rodin sculpture, *The Thinker?* There were people who criticized it. They said that Rodin could only make big sculptures. So Rodin made a small *Thinker*. Carlos has it. At the time of the event he was in the process of constructing a museum in the name of his wife to house his collection so that he could share it with all of Mexico. When he spoke about it, there was something in his tone that was strangely familiar, so familiar that I almost didn't recognize it at first. Then it hit me. He spoke about the art with the same pride that you'd hear in my voice if I were walking you through my trophy room. My trophies aren't trophies. They're all memories that tell me something about life.

Dinner was scheduled for ten o'clock that night. When I told Carlos that I don't stay up late, he moved it up to eight o'clock. I hadn't brought a tie on the trip. I was the only one in a large group who showed up at dinner without a tie. Carlos took off his tie.

I had so many questions to ask him.

You own so many companies. How do you stay on top of them all?

After you buy ten suits, how can you be just as curious about the eleventh? How do you maintain your interest?

I was thrilled when he agreed to come on my show. The little kid in me has always pinched myself when I get to meet people like Carlos. And when I hear that Carlos Slim is pinching himself in order to believe he's meeting me, it makes me pinch myself again. Is this reality?

There was a movie made years ago about reality, perception, and money that I really love. It stars Gregory Peck and it's called *The Million Pound Note.*

Peck plays this down-and-out American sailor on a fourteen-foot cutter who gets lost in a gale and is picked up by a British steamer. He arrives in London penniless and shabby, in need of a job. He's walking down the street when two rich men see him. They make a bet. One says that simply giving Peck a million-pound note will lead him to riches and fame. The idea is that Peck wouldn't even have to cash it—the aura of the note would bring him wealth. The other man bets that there's no way the note could make Peck what he wasn't.

So they call him in and give him this envelope. They tell him if he wants a job he must bring back what's inside the envelope in thirty days. If he doesn't bring it back, he'll be out on the street again. They don't give him anything else. All Gregory Peck has got as he goes out the door is this envelope.

He hasn't had a meal for a while and goes into a fancy London restaurant. Naturally, the staff doesn't want such a shabby guy inside. But he gets a table and eats. When it's time to pay the bill, he opens up the envelope and is shocked to find the million-pound note.

He gives it to the waiter to pay his bill. Of course, the restaurant doesn't have the cash on hand to break it. The staff assumes Peck is an eccentric millionaire and begins bowing to him. *No charge at all, sir.* They're delighted merely to be in his presence. *Please, come back anytime.*

The subplot is he meets a wonderful girl who doesn't realize he's wealthy and falls for him. Everyone else is mesmerized by the note. Peck goes to a swanky hotel and it's *Right this way, sir.* He goes to a tailor shop, is measured and outfitted. The bills keep mounting, but nobody asks him to pay.

When the girl hears that he's rich, that he's not who she thought, she leaves him. But word of his wealth attracts everyone else. He becomes a front man for a gold mine. People invest in the mine simply on the strength of his recommendation, which has merit only because of the note.

Then the note is stolen, and people start getting suspicious. Just as an angry mob of investors converges on him, the guy who took the note returns, raises it for all to see and saves his reputation. There's a happy twist: The girl comes back when she finds out that Peck is the regular guy she'd fallen for in the first place. In the end you're back at the beginning. You're left to wonder: What is wealth? The way you're seen, or who you actually are?

The movie came to mind when I was told about a funny situation Carlos got into when he arrived in L.A. to appear on my show. Carlos didn't want the interview to be overly serious, so he thought he'd inject a little surprise by wearing colorful suspenders. He didn't bring any with him from Mexico, so he decided to buy a pair. Easy enough. Carlos is the majority shareholder of Saks Inc., the parent company of Saks Fifth Avenue. So he goes to visit the one in the heart of Beverly Hills.

Everybody at Saks, his assistant is thinking, is going to faint when they realize the owner is in the building.

"Of course not," Carlos tells her, "nobody's going to even recognize me."

He walks in and, sure enough, nobody has any idea that the owner is on his way to the men's department. He's certainly not dressed as shabbily as Gregory Peck coming off the boat—but you get the irony. He owns the store and everybody he passes assumes he's just an ordinary shopper.

A salesman comes over to him in the men's department. Carlos asks to see some colored suspenders.

The sales guy says, "Well, we've got some nice white ones. But if you really want colorful suspenders, you should go to this store two blocks away. They've got a great selection there."

The assistant is standing behind Carlos—so Carlos can't see her. Her eyes are squinched shut. She's gritting her teeth. Her head is furiously shaking back and forth. Silently, she's trying to save the salesman's job: No, no, no!

But the sales guy is adamant. "It's a great shop. You'll see, they offer everything you'd ever want to see in suspenders."

Carlos is very calm. "Yes," he says. "But I'd like to find the suspenders here."

"I'm telling you," the guy says. "You don't want to buy suspenders here. Take my word for it, go to this other shop."

"I'm sorry," Carlos says. "But do you work for Saks? Or do you work for this other store?"

"Of course I work for Saks," the salesman says. "But I don't want to waste your time."

So Carlos convinces the salesman to sell him a pair of white suspenders. Never tells the guy who he is. Then he goes to the other store. Why? Because he's a businessman and he wants to see what his own store is lacking and why his own salesman would send him elsewhere. Just as the salesman suggested, that's where he ends up buying the colorful suspenders.

You walk away from the story the way you walk away from the Gregory Peck movie: with questions. Was the sales guy working against his own company? Would the customer never again see Saks as his first option for shopping? Or did the sales guy help the store in the long run? Would the customer return to the men's department at Saks to buy something else simply because he trusted the sales guy's recommendations? In the end, both the movie and the story have little to do with money. They're about something much deeper. Which is exactly what made me so proud of my interview with Carlos Slim. By the end of that hour, anybody who tuned in could no longer see Carlos Slim as a number. They saw him for the man he truly is.

He employs 250,000 people in Central America. He runs his businesses with austerity—no frills during the boom times. Until recently, there were no corporate headquarters. Management had their offices in individual factories. His goal is to distribute income so that it will lift the entire region. Owning thirty cars or forty watches has no meaning to him. He compares it to buying toy after toy for a child who's too busy opening the wrapping paper to ever play with the first one. When we met he was financing 120,000 surgeries a year. I have an idea of what that means to him, because my cardiac foundation saves a life almost every day. Both Carlos and I have had open-heart surgery. It's jokingly called the Zipper Club. It's an exclusive group: people who've had a surgeon physically touch their heart understand each other—and their time—in a way that others never will.

I didn't tell Carlos about some of the guests I'd invited before he came for dinner. I'll never forget the childlike look of astonishment on his face when he whispered, "Is that Ernie Banks?"

The evening was surreal. The Chicago Cubs great was in my home. And there was Carlos Slim, in a catcher's stance imitating Yogi Berra and receiving a pitch from the mayor of Los Angeles. My eleven-year-old, Chance, was casually talking to the all-time home-run record holder, Barry Bonds. As I looked on, I could imagine myself running down the street by Ebbets Field following the Dodgers after games. Not for autographs. I just wanted to ask them questions. *Why did you bunt in the fifth inning?* Chance has been in the Dodgers dugout many, many times. Tommy Lasorda once carried out his birthday cake at spring training. Now he was listening to Barry Bonds talk about hitting strategy as if it were simply an interesting conversation. Did he even understand the life that he was living? Or was that impossible? Because, to him, it was normal.

To me, wealth was the evening. Wealth was having Sidney Poitier read this poem written by my youngest son, Cannon.

Portrait of My Dad

When my dad is late, his eyes are like burning fire
    moving furiously in a black pot.
Oh, Dad, you are a clock screaming let's go with a
    gnarled voice in the morning sky.
Sometimes, you are a baseball flying to different ball-
    parks in the night sky.
Other times, you are an ocean flowing with the wind
    and the fish.
One thing I really like about you is your sport com-
    petivity. It runs every day with excitement.
Oh, Dad, you are a clock screaming let's go with a
    gnarled voice in the morning sky.
Without you, the world would break in pieces and the
    sun would never shine on Earth.
Oh, Dad, you are a clock screaming let's go with a
    gnarled voice in the morning sky.

I looked around and saw friends. My producer, Wendy, Ryan Seacrest, and a long table of others. Wolfgang Puck was in the kitchen cooking. Every time I wondered how the evening could possibly improve, it got better.

Toward the end of the dinner, Shawn noticed that the conversations were clustering at different parts of the table. She thought it would be good if everyone could come together. So I got up and said, "Thanksgiving has just passed. I'd like to ask everyone at the table to take a moment and tell us what they're thankful for."

Sidney Poitier told this amazing story of his unexpected and premature birth. He was born while his mother and father were in Miami to sell a hundred boxes of tomatoes they'd grown back in the Bahamas. And he came out weighing less than three pounds. His father had already lost several children to disease and stillbirth. So he went to the undertaker in the "colored" section of Miami and came back with a shoebox for a casket. But his mother went to a fortune-teller who said the shoebox wouldn't be necessary. "Don't worry about your son," the fortune-teller said. "He will travel to the corners of the earth and walk with kings." The story went on for twelve minutes. These few sentences do his eloquence little justice.

Everybody's reflections were moving—and nobody mentioned money. Seventy-nine year old Ernie Banks and his wife gave thanks for being able to recently adopt a two-year-old. It turns out that Carlos's assistant was born very late to her parents and didn't grow up with much family. She gave thanks that Carlos's son would call her "cousin." Shawn was nearly crying as she spoke about her parents, who had helped her through what had been a very tough year. The mood of the room became so intimate that the servers could sense it and they stopped coming in.

Carlos asked to be left to the end. I noticed him writing some notes as the others spoke and I saw how seriously he takes what he says even at a dinner party. He wanted to make sure his words were as meaningful as the gift he brought Shawn: his wife's favorite serving plate. In the best way he could, he'd brought his wife to the dinner.

The biggest commitment that he has with himself, Carlos said, is to learn something different every day. He doesn't want a day to go by without learning something new. He wanted to thank us for having given him the opportunity to learn so many new things.

"This," he said, "has been one of the most memorable days in my life."

At age seventy-seven, I was still making friends like Carlos Slim. Which made me feel like the richest man in the world.

4

Music

Musicians were guests on many of the shows that aired over my last two weeks. Jon Bon Jovi brought along a pair of bright red suspenders for me to wear on my final show. Celine Dion sang John Lennon's "Imagine." Barbra Streisand opened up her home. Garth Brooks took the time to talk with people on our staff in a way that made them feel as special as he is. Stevie Wonder composed a song for me. It had a rhyme I wasn't quite expecting.

Larry, I'm gonna miss ya.
If you were a woman, I'd kiss ya.

I've always had an affinity for musicians. I've never really thought of this until now, but in a way it was a musician who gave me my start—or at least a sense of what I was to become. The first celebrity I ever interviewed was a singer. I never even asked for the interview. Bobby Darin just showed up one morning out of the blue.

I'd just left my first job for another station. The new station worked out a deal for me to broadcast live from a deli in
Miami Beach called Pumpernik's. The hour after breakfast was
slow at the restaurant, and the owner figured the show might
bring some traffic. It was a very simple setup. After the early
morning broadcast from the station, I walked over to the deli
and picked the show up from there. The deli had an elevated
platform with a table, a couple of chairs, and a microphone—
that was it. Jerry Seinfeld said that when he watched *Larry
King Live* he always felt like the show was coming from a deli.
That's probably because my style was formed at Pumpernik's.
I hadn't done much interviewing before then. All of a sudden
I was talking to anyone who came over—waiters, plumbers,
conventioneers. An eight-year-old kid could venture over to the
microphone. Anything could happen. There was no way to
prepare. I never knew who was going to be in front of me.
Fifty-three years later, my ideal guest would still be someone
interesting who walks over and surprises me.

After about two weeks, Darin walked in. He had trouble
sleeping at night, and he'd heard me promote the show from
the studio early that morning. I loved "Mack the Knife" but I
really didn't know anything about him. We spoke for an hour
on the air, then took a long walk along the beach. Darin started
confiding in me. He was born with a rheumatic heart and he
knew he wasn't going to live a long life, so he tried to pack
everything he could into every single day. The conversation
was the kind you'd have with an old friend. It was as if, on that
day, he showed me the music that was inside me.

* * *

Musicians are always giving us gifts. One of the best is that they can bring us back in time and make us feel young again. At breakfast the other day, I recalled a song that Bob Marley sang. It was called "Kaya." I have a daughter whose name is pronounced the same—Chaia. As I was telling the story, I could see my daughter singing that song. I was back in the moment. I could hear Chaia's eight-year-old voice. "Got to have ka-ya now . . ." She loved that song—and had no idea that it was about marijuana.

Then my mind flashed ahead and I could picture exactly where Bob Marley was sitting when I interviewed him. I could see him right down to the beads in his dreadlocks.

Then my mind fast-forwarded years later to a college kid who asked me in disbelief: You met *Bob Marley?*

Well, of course I met Bob Marley. It was no big deal. He was doing a concert in Miami, we gave him a call and he came over to talk.

You met Bob Marley?

As if Bob Marley was from another century. Then it hit me. *It was* another century. Chaia is not eight years old anymore—she's forty-three. Bob Marley has been dead for thirty years. And not only did I meet Bob Marley, I met Louie Armstrong! As soon as I snap away from the warmth of those moments, I feel old. And do you know what old feels like? Old is when you ask George Burns if he's got arthritis and he replies: "I was the first."

It's a strange sensation, to be swept back in time in one instant, then feel ancient the next. I don't know if I can describe it. Maybe you have to be in my shoes—but maybe not. Maybe I can get the feeling across simply by telling stories about many of the musicians I've met and the music they've made. That way, you'll be back in all those moments with me. And when you add them up, you'll see what I mean.

America the Beautiful

Songs come up randomly. This is a good one to begin with. I don't think I ever heard a better rendition of "America the Beautiful" than Ray Charles's. It's more than a good singer singing a good song. Ray went beyond the song. Here's what amazes me about it. The America that Ray Charles grew up in was not a beautiful place—not if you were black.

There was nobody better than a blind man to show how ridiculous it is to discriminate because of skin color. He told me a story that's so sad it's funny. He remembered going to a school for the blind as a boy in Florida. At this school, the white kids were placed on one side of the room and the black kids on the other. They couldn't see each other's skin color. But they were separated.

I've always wondered if he needed to be blind to sing "America the Beautiful" the way he did. He knew prejudice— but he didn't see it. Maybe if he'd seen it, the song would have come out differently.

Day-O

Harry Belafonte's voice reminds me of the day he changed everything on Miami Beach.

I went to set up an interview with him at a new hotel where he was going to perform. Jackie Gleason owned a piece of this hotel. Black entertainers worked in Miami Beach in the early sixties—but they never stayed in Miami Beach. They weren't allowed. They stayed at the Sir John, a swank hotel in the black area of Miami.

Harry was going to open Friday. On Tuesday, he arrived for rehearsals and walked to the hotel counter to check in.

"Hello, Mr. Belafonte," the clerk says. "So excited to have you here. We have a car to take you to the Sir John where you'll be staying."

Harry says, "Why am I staying at the Sir John?"

"That's where our Negro entertainers stay."

Harry says, "Not this one. I stay where I work. I'm not working at the Sir John, and I'm not staying at the Sir John."

There's a panic behind the desk. Calls are made. Finally, they get Gleason on the phone. "What kind of bullshit is this?" Jackie says. "Check him in."

"OK." The clerk turns to Harry and says, "We'll make an exception for you."

This was huge. I ran to the pay phone to call the *Miami Herald*. It was gigantic news—and Harry wouldn't stop pushing it.

"I'm with twelve people," he says. "Six men and six women. They sing and dance behind me. They stay where they play, too."

It was like Jackie Robinson bringing in a whole team of black ballplayers to a ballfield that had never allowed blacks to play.

All the singers and dancers were checked in. Reporters started running in from all over. Everybody was going crazy. The feeling in the lobby that day is impossible for a young person today to imagine.

Malice in Wonderland

We taped an hour with the rapper Snoop Dogg last summer. I drove around in his car—a '67 Pontiac. The paint job cost twenty-five grand. We had cornbread, chicken and waffles. It was a blast. Fog machines were going when he walked on the set.

When the taping was over, Snoop left just before the Republican presidential candidate Mitt Romney came in to do the live show.

When Romney heard he'd just missed Snoop Dogg he couldn't believe it. "Ohhhhh," he said, "I really wanted to meet him."

The two of them together—that's a picture I'd like to have.

I'd lived through Nat King Cole not being able to have his show televised in the South. I can remember when Joe Kennedy wouldn't let Sammy Davis Jr. sing at President Kennedy's inaugural. And I've seen Mitt Romney upset that he didn't get to meet Snoop Dogg.

Did all this really happen in a single lifetime?

Hello, Dolly!

I'm always amazed where music comes from. There are probably more melodies than there are grains of sand in the desert—each containing its own story. Many of those stories are too mysterious to be understood. It was useless to ask Louie Armstrong about his music. "I don't know what I do," he told me, "I just know that I do it."

Ma Cherie Amour

It's my favorite Stevie Wonder song. I never get tired of it. Ask him where his music comes from, and he'll tell you he's simply the vehicle for a higher power. But that higher power seems to delight in throwing down obstacles to make the music better.

Stevie told me that when he first wrote the song, it was about his girlfriend. It was called "My Marsha—I Wish That You Were Mine."

But then he and Marsha broke up.

I Walk the Line

Everything about this song came backward. Johnny Cash told me he decided to record a melody he'd been strumming on his guitar. He was using a Wilcox-Gay recorder—the kind popular in the Air Force back in the fifties. Somehow he inserted the tape backward and when he replayed the melody and the sound came through the speakers he couldn't figure out how he'd done it. The sound kept haunting him—just wouldn't leave his mind. Then he put words to it: "Because you're mine, I walk the line."

He didn't think the song was any good. He was on tour the first time he heard it on the radio, and he immediately called Sun Records and begged them to stop making the record. "Please don't send it out to any more radio stations," he said. "I just don't want to hear it anymore."

"Well," he was told, "you'll have to keep your radio off because it's playing everywhere."

In another week it was number one.

Best That You Can Do

Peter Allen told me how he was struck by the inspiration for the theme song to the movie *Arthur*. He was flying into New York one night—a beautiful night. He could see the moon. Bright stars. But he couldn't see the city because of a very low layer of clouds below. The pilot said, "We're going to have to circle a few times."

Peter took out a pencil and wrote: *When you get caught between the moon and New York City.*

God Bless America

Irving Berlin didn't like it when he wrote it. He put it away in a drawer, and it stayed there for twenty years. Then one day, Kate Smith called him up. She had a July 4 show coming up. The conversation went something like this.

"Irving, you got something?"

"I wrote something a long time ago, but it's no good—too sentimental."

"Let me see it."

"I don't like it."

"Let me see it . . ."

The Christmas Song
(Chestnuts Roasting on an Open Fire)

It was ninety-five degrees in Chicago and the air conditioner was broken in the hotel. Mel Tormé told me he wrote that song just so he could think of something cold.

Ac-Cent-Tchu-Ate the Positive

Johnny Mercer never wrote a lyric before he got the tune. He had Harold Arlen's tune in his head when he walked into an elevator. Then the elevator got stuck.

Misty

Erroll Garner played piano in a very distinctive style. Never took a lesson. He was in a car with a friend. They were driving along and Earl started singing this melody.

The friend said, "That's pretty."

Garner said, "I heard it somewhere on the radio."

They drove a little further and Garner kept taking the melody forward.

"You sure you heard that song?" the friend said.

"I guess. It's in my head."

"Why don't we write that down?"

Earl didn't know he'd composed a song. Music just swirled through him.

Yesterday

Eric Clapton tells the story about going backstage to meet the Beatles for the first time. Paul McCartney was strumming a beautiful melody on the guitar. He didn't have the lyrics yet. He was singing: *Scrambled eggs . . . everybody calls me scrambled eggs.*

"Stupid words," he said. "But what do you think?"

I Write the Songs

Ever go to a Barry Manilow show? Every song has the emotion of a closing number.

An interesting thing about Manilow: He was famous for singing "I Write the Songs." But he didn't write that one. Bruce Johnston of the Beach Boys did.

Take the "A" Train

Not many people know it, but Duke Ellington also wrote a Catholic mass.

Oh, What a Beautiful Morning

This comes from the play *Oklahoma!* written by Richard Rodgers and Oscar Hammerstein. Not much was expected from the show. The play was a remake of a western that opened up on Broadway in the thirties.

The songs were beautiful, but one of the critics noted that the first one didn't come until fifteen minutes into the show.

So Rodgers and Hammerstein went to their hotel room and wrote "Oh, What a Beautiful Morning." They couldn't restage the play. So they just had the male lead, Curly, open the show by walking out onstage and singing.

When you see a musical now, with the music completely integrated into the plot, you know where it comes from.

I Will Always Love You

Whitney Houston made it famous. But it was Dolly Parton's song. When I asked Dolly if she liked hearing other people sing her songs, she said it was thrilling.

The first time she heard Whitney sing it she thought, "Is that my little song?"

But that's how you know a song is special. Like Stevie Wonder says, a song is great when it opens itself to various interpretations.

MacArthur Park

This was a Jimmy Webb song. Sinatra loved Jimmy Webb, and Sinatra was crazy about lyrics. He used to talk about lyrics all the time—dissected every lyric he sang.

But he could never get "MacArthur Park."

Frank said, " 'Someone left the cake out in the rain . . .' What the hell does that mean?"

Remember

Luciano Pavarotti told me that singing was much more than having a great voice. He said his father had a better voice than he did. But that was all his father had. It's how you use the voice, Pavarotti explained. It's the phrasing and the intonations that bring a personality to the voice so that it can't be confused with any other.

There are a lot of pretty voices that can't sell a song.

They're just pretty. But when you hear *You got to win . . . a little. Lose . . . a little,* you know it can't be anybody else but Jimmy Durante. It's not only the voice; his personality comes out in the pauses, too.

Once, when he was having difficulty with a song, Sinatra called Pavarotti for advice. Pavarotti didn't know the song. So Frank sang it for him. It was called "Remember" by Irving Berlin.

Frank sang it smooth. "No," Pavarotti, told him. "It's an angry song. *This-a* guy *is-a* pissed. So hit the *b* in "remember." Instead of remember, make it remem-*ber*.

It's those little things . . .

Bat out of Hell

This song reminds me of a good time I had with Bob Costas. This was when he was doing the *Later with Bob Costas* show. I told him how my dream interview is "Good evening . . . ," then the door opens and I discover who the guest is.

Bob and I decided to get surprise guests for each other— no prep. They just walk in. So I sent him Mario Cuomo. And Mario was great because he was one-wording Bob at the start. "Yes . . . No." Just to make it difficult.

Bob sent me a guy I'd never seen before. The guy walked on the set, and I had no idea who he was. So I asked him his name. He said, "Meatloaf."

I said, "When you check into a hotel, do they call you Mr. Loaf?"

Silent Night

Talk about an entrance. I'll never forget when I first met Barbra Streisand. She was relatively unknown and singing at the

Eden Roc in Miami Beach. Her manager called me up and said, "Nobody's coming. The waiters are standing on the tables applauding, but nobody else is here. Will you put her on the radio?"

The producers weren't impressed: "Just another pretty face." But they booked her.

Barbra said something before that first interview that remains etched in my mind almost fifty years later. "I know you don't know me. But you are going to know me, Larry King, you are going to know me."

"Silent Night" is Barbra at the top of her game. A Catholic priest once told me Barbra's "Silent Night" was the best ever done.

A-Tisket, A-Tasket

Ella Fitzgerald was like a housewife, your neighbor down the street. What a nice lady. And boy could she sing.

Streisand told me she wouldn't have dared follow Ella in concert.

The Kid from Red Bank

I love this Count Basie story. It's a big night—Sinatra opens at the Fontainebleau. Count Basie's band is playing. As Sinatra starts singing, he notices that Basie has music in front of him at the piano.

What's going on? Sinatra wonders. Basie never uses sheet music. The arrangements are in his head. Basie just plunked away in that very distinctive style. What the hell is Basie doing with sheet music? Frank works his way down the stage. He gets behind the piano and takes a closer look.

It's not sheet music. Basie's got the *Racing Form* opened up and he's analyzing the next day's races.

At the next break, Frank goes over to Basie and asks him about it. "What are you doing?"

And Basie says, "I can do more than one thing at once, you know."

Now, that's my definition of confidence. "When you sing with Basie, the band propels you," Frank told me. "If you can't sing with Basie, you can't sing."

This Land Is Your Land

Pete Seeger was called a Communist when he was with a group called the Weavers. When he was called to testify before the HUAC hearings, Seeger refused to answer and was convicted of contempt. I asked him, Who is the greatest American hero?

He said, "American?"

I said, "Yes, specifically American."

"Geronimo."

Seeger explained: Geronimo was a pure American hero. He fought against invaders. He was a genius tactician. Anybody who ever fought against him marveled at his techniques. Plus, he's saluted every time a guy jumps out of an airplane.

Begin the Beguine

This was one of the greatest musical arrangements of all time. Artie Shaw was a genius. He married Lana Turner and dated

Rita Hayworth. I think he married eight times. Artie stopped playing clarinet at age fifty-four. I asked him why, and he said, *I have nothing more to say.*

He lived for another half century, taught students, did interviews, but he never played his instrument again. If there wasn't anything new to say, he didn't want to say anything.

The Way We Were

I had Marvin Hamlisch on my radio show one night for five and a half hours. He answered questions, played songs, even wrote songs on the air.

Marvin was a prodigy. A lot of times prodigies don't go very far because they know more than their teachers—so they aren't pushed. Marvin kept getting better.

There was something special about him on the piano. Garth Brooks told me a story about being at an event where several piano players followed each other. When Marvin touched the keys, it was as if somebody had brought in a new piano. It felt to Garth like the piano was breathing and bending around Marvin's fingers.

"That's the difference between owning an instrument and mastering one," Garth said. "When you heard Marvin play, you wanted to sob."

Light My Fire

I had Jim Morrison on the show the night after he was arrested in Miami. What a handsome guy. His father was an admiral, and he was a rebellious poet. He died in a bathtub of a drug overdose.

You know what I think of when I hear "Light My Fire"? My childhood pal Asher Dann. Asher managed Jim at one point. They had fistfights. Knock down, drag out fights.

Now Jim is buried in Paris. And there are days when you'll find Asher wearing a neck brace having breakfast at Nate 'n Al's.

Chances Are

Johnny Mathis had one of the most romantic voices of all time. When he did concerts, the women would crush up against the stage. Johnny would walk along the stage holding out his hotel key while the girls tried to grab it.

For some reason, the program director at WIOD in Miami did not share this passion for Johnny Mathis's voice. Harry Ballows hated Johnny Mathis's voice. Couldn't stand it!

A lot of radio stations are formatted these days. The music is predetermined. But back then, a lot of disc jockeys could play whatever they wanted. So whenever we saw Harry Ballows walking down the hall, we'd put on a Johnny Mathis tune. As soon as he heard, "Chances are . . ." he'd cup his hands over his ears, press down as hard as he could, and run for it.

We played Johnny every time we saw him.

I Left My Heart in San Francisco

Tony Bennett is the most amazing of all. He perpetually stays on top. He's eighty-four, and he sings every day. Many of his concerts have a unique close. He puts the mike down and sings a cappella. You really feel the power of his voice.

This song always reminds me of my recovery following heart surgery. A brain surgeon came over to wish me well while I was still in the hospital. Then he started to complain. He said, "These heart surgeons. Everyone sees them as heroes, but they're really all plumbers. They move things around. That's it. But brain surgery, that's different. We have to act with infinite skill. One slight movement with our hand can affect your memory. We have to be delicate. We are the definition of precision. And nobody knows!"

I said, "Hey, the song ain't 'I Left My Brain in San Francisco.'"

Rhythm Is Gonna Get You

There are certain voices that remind you of places. The Miami Dolphins brought me back to a game last year to honor me. They let me announce a quarter of the game over the radio. Gloria Estefan was there. She gave me a big hug. It was like going home again.

New York State of Mind

If you're away from New York and want to feel like you're back home, this is the song you play.

Honey in the Horn

They used to call Al Hirt the Round Mound of Sound. He used to tell me stories about leaving his club in the French Quarter of New Orleans at two in the morning and walking down the street with his band. At the same time, Pete Fountain would leave his club with his band. All the musicians would meet and walk down the streets playing music.

Way Down Yonder in New Orleans

Years ago, I was king of the Mardi Gras in New Orleans. They make a special outfit for you with a crown. They make special doubloons with your face on it and you toss them to the crowds. At the end of the motorcade is breakfast at 3 a.m.

I can remember walking with Brad Pitt through areas still devastated by Hurricane Katrina. Brad and Angelina Jolie had moved there and were helping to restore the city.

When I think of those moments, I can hear Harry Connick Jr.'s voice.

Graceland

I don't know why this South African rhythm resonated with me so much. That's one of the great things about Paul Simon. He's always looking for a new place to take you.

Blue Skies

The last time Willie Nelson came on my show, I asked him if he'd smoked pot that day. He said, "Right before the show."

Birth of the Blues

When Sammy Davis Jr. was at the height of his career, he had a sign on his dressing room in Vegas that said PLEASE SMOKE.

I interviewed him after he found out he had cancer. "It's been a blessing," he told me, "a miracle. I know I can't drink now. I know I can't smoke. I'm going to lead a clean life. I've got to live, man." He was crying, thanking all the people who were supporting him.

Afterward, he went back to the green room where my friend George Schlatter was waiting for him. George said as soon as he got there, Sammy drank a water glass full of booze and lit up a Pall Mall.

"Sammy," George said, "you just told Larry you had a miracle."

"I know," Sammy said. "I'll quit tomorrow."

School's Out for Summer

Alice Cooper is not what you see onstage. His wild dress in concert belies what he is: a good golfer.

The Lawrence Welk Show Theme

Lawrence Welk was such a bad host that you couldn't stop watching the show. He was so bad that he was good. In all the years, he never learned how to host.

But the great clarinet player Pete Fountain always gave Lawrence Welk a lot of credit. He said what Welk taught him was discipline. When you played in Welk's band, you rehearsed at a precise time. You played the tune exactly the way it was designed. For a Dixieland player like Fountain, that was very important.

Escapade

Not only did I once dance with Janet Jackson, but she gave me suspenders with the nipples cut out.

On the Street Where You Live

This is a song from *My Fair Lady*. I love it when it's sung by Vic Damone. Sinatra always said, "I wish I had Vic Damone's voice." He was envious—that a guy could just go out and sing like that. And Vic would rather play golf.

I sat at Vic's desk at Lafayette High School a few years after him. It was art class. I know it was Vic's desk because he carved his name into it: Vito Farinola.

Unforgettable

Natalie Cole came on the show a couple of years ago and told the world that she was alive only because of dialysis. She had difficulty breathing. Her kidney functions were at 8 percent. She needed a transplant.

Now get this: A nurse was watching the show with her niece, who was in the hospital dying from complications of childbirth. The nurse and the niece both agreed that it would be great to give Natalie a kidney. When the niece died, her kidney was donated to Natalie.

Natalie came back on the show months later with the aunt and the sister of the donor. It all came about because of the show. That's hard to top.

My Heart Will Go On

On a special we once did, celebrities talked about their favorite moments on the show.

Celine Dion said her favorite memory was doing the show for the first time. She said her husband had told her, "The day you do *Larry King* is the day you're going to be a star." So she was really nervous.

I had no idea. It reminded me that something had happened to me along the way. I used to be so proud when people in Miami told Miles Davis: "You gotta go on with the kid"—meaning me. It was a symbol to me of how far I'd come. Then it sort of flipped around. I'd become a symbol of how far *they'd* come.

Michael Bublé got his break on my show. His grandmother was a huge fan of the show. Michael said she wasn't going to believe it when she saw him on *Larry King Live*. So my producer, Greg Christensen, said: "Hey, why don't we call her?" I phoned her from the makeup room. Michael was in the hallway holding his chest as if he were having a heart attack.

La Vida Loca

Ricky Martin played at my cardiac foundation gala right after "La Vida Loca" came out. You couldn't have been bigger than

Ricky Martin at the time. We were in the elevator at the Ritz-Carlton, and when the door opened, we were mobbed by a sea of girls. We couldn't get out of the elevator. It was like a wave of energy crashing in on us.

I thought about that when he came on my show last year to discuss his decision to tell the world that he's gay. That took a lot of courage. He could have kept it to himself. But his decision made sense. He said his lowest moments were when he saw gays being put down. It pained him to not do anything about it when he knew he had the power to help make a change.

Born in the USA

I've interviewed everybody once. How did I miss Bruce Springsteen?

Hero

I didn't know what to expect when I heard Mariah Carey was coming on the show. At the time, Mariah had the most number-one-selling singles of any solo artist—and that included Elvis. But she also had an image as a pampered diva. AT&T even played off that image in a commercial.

Let me tell you something: Mariah Carey is a good time. Do you know how you can get a feeling for people by the way they react with your friends? I got a feeling for Mariah by the way she hit it off with one of my oldest pals, Sid Young.

We were doing the show at the studio in New York and Sid happened to be outside the elevator when she stepped out.

Of course, Sid knew she was going to be the guest. But he's

always up for a little fun. He'd be perfect on Ashton Kutcher's show *Punk'd*. Sid said in dumbfounded innocence, "Gee, you look like Mariah Carey."

She said, "I *am* Mariah Carey."

"C'mon . . ."

"*Really*, I am."

Sid waved his hand in her face. "Don't mess around with me." He always does this, and the way he does it is perfect. He once had Oprah Winfrey believing he had no idea who she was for five minutes and trying to explain to him how Oprah really was her first name.

"*Honest!*" Mariah said. She was almost about to take out her driver's license to prove it—which is as far from a diva as she could possibly get. "I'm here to be interviewed by Larry King."

Finally, Sid started cracking up and they hugged each other.

You get an idea why Sid is one of the great friends in the history of the world. There isn't anybody who Sid isn't friends with.

In fact, there's a slightly embellished story about Sid that explains just how popular he is. Many years back, he was playing golf with a man he'd recently met. After making a beautiful shot, Sid says: "That's very similar to the shot I hit with Eisenhower last week."

The guy felt he was getting put on. So he says: "Sid, I'll bet you $10,000 you don't know Dwight Eisenhower."

So they flew to Pennsylvania and rang the bell at Eisenhower's house. The door opens. Eisenhower comes out. "Sid!" Ike hugs him. "You gotta stay! You gotta stay!"

The other golfer is deflated. They leave Eisenhower's house a few hours later. Once they get out the door, the other guy feels he's been taken. He says, "I can't believe it. The one guy you knew. Eisenhower. It's a good thing you hadn't hit that shot and said you'd played with de Gaulle."

Sid says, "Chuck? An old buddy of mine."

The other golfer was having none of it. They bet double or nothing. They flew to France. Sid took him to de Gaulle's house. They ring the bell. From the top of the stairs, de Gaulle slides down the banister. "Sidney, my old friend!"

Now the golf partner is totally whipped. He says, "There's gotta be somebody you don't know. I'll bet you don't know the pope."

Sid says, "One of my best friends."

They go to the Vatican. Ring the bell. They tell one of the cardinals that Sid Young was there to see the pope.

The cardinal comes back and says, "Only Sid. No one else."

So the golfing partner says, "Wait a minute, Sid! You could have set all this up with the cardinal in advance. How can I be sure?"

So Sid says, "Tell you what. I'll go on the veranda with the pope and we'll wave down to you."

The friend goes outside. Sid comes out on the veranda. There's a guy with him. The guy's dressed in a robe and that tall white peaked hat. They have their arms around each other.

The other golfer's wondering: *Could this be fake?*

A group of nuns is walking by, and he asks if any of them speaks English.

One says, "I do."

"Can you do me a favor?" the golfer says.

"Sure."

"Can you tell me, is that the pope?"

The nun squints. "The sun is right in my eyes," she says. "I can't tell. But the guy with him is Sid Young."

The moral of the story is, don't ever bet Mariah Carey that she doesn't know Sid Young.

Poker Face

Lady Gaga reminds you that there's always going to be something new. Gaga told me she's constantly thinking of unique ways to shock and annoy people.

I wonder what she thought when she heard Ryan Seacrest and me doing a duet of "Poker Face."

Coca-Cola Cowboy

Mel Tillis is the only singer I know who stutters—except when he's singing. Hearing Mel sing always reminds me of that old joke about the comic and the stuttering singer living together in a hotel room. The comic comes in, and the singer says: "W-w-w-w . . . w-w-w-w-w . . ."

The comic says, "Sing!"

The singer sings, "We've been robbed!"

Gone Too Soon

Anybody who was at Michael Jackson's memorial service will never forget Usher singing "Gone Too Soon."

The thing most people don't know about Usher is that this guy really knows his politics.

Melancholy Baby

Bing Crosby's at the racetrack. He runs into Joe Frisco. Joe was a comedian who used a violin and his stutter as part of his act.

Joe tells Bing, "I g-g-g-got no money. C-c-can you loan me a hundred?"

Bing loans him a hundred.

Later that day, Bing is on his way to the restroom and he sees Joe Frisco sitting at a table with four women and a tub of champagne. They're eating a lavish meal and Joe Frisco is having the time of his life.

Bing can't believe it. A guy notices the look of incredulity on Bing's face and tells Bing what happened: "Joe Frisco hit the big daily double. Made a fortune."

Crosby says, "I'm going to embarrass him. I'm going to go over and ask for my money."

Bing approaches the table and says, "You got my hundred?"

Frisco pulls a hundred out of his pocket and says, "S-s-s-s-sing 'Melancholy Baby.'"

Candle in the Wind

Elton John sang it at Princess Diana's funeral service. He told me it was the hardest thing he ever had to do in music.

He'd sung the song about Marilyn Monroe many times, and had just rewritten the lyric for Di. He was terrified that he'd forget the new words and sing "Goodbye Norma Jean," in front of billions of people, so he had a teleprompter set in front of him to remind him.

Long Day's Journey

Nobody could play like Buddy Rich. Mel Tormé told me he wanted to play the drums until he heard Buddy. Then he threw away the sticks. Sinatra loved Buddy too. There is a wonderful story about Buddy and Frank that Al Pacino likes to tell.

Al goes to a Sinatra concert. Buddy Rich is the opening act. Al knows Buddy is a good drummer, but Buddy's in his sixties at that point and Al's thinking: I'll listen for a little while, twiddle my thumbs, and wait for Frank.

Buddy comes on, gets going and keeps going . . . and going . . . and going. He goes way beyond anything Al thought he was going to do and he keeps going after that. And it becomes this *experience*. Al can feel it, and everyone else can, too. Because the entire audience jumps to its feet simultaneously and starts screaming. And Buddy just keeps on going. It was as if he was saying, I went this far, lemme see if I can take it further. And then suddenly it takes itself.

When it was over, Sinatra came out and said, "You see this guy drumming? You know, sometimes it's a good idea to stay at a thing."

Don't Be Cruel

I never met Elvis. Never saw him in concert. But there are at least three times I wish I could have been around him.

The first is when he came to Miami Beach to do a concert at the convention center. He was helicoptered in and then driven over in a limo. At the end of his stay, he asked the driver, "Is this your car?"

The driver says, "No, I just drive it."

Elvis says, "It is now. It's your tip."

I'd have loved to see that driver's face.

Then there's the great story that's just as much about Jerry Weintraub as it is about Elvis. Jerry is a guy who can talk as well as Elvis could sing. Business is a creative art to Jerry. He takes huge risks—which always makes for the best stories.

One night back in the midsixties, Jerry wakes up with an idea to take Elvis on tour.

Problem is, Elvis isn't touring at that point. He's making movies. But that doesn't deter Jerry. Jerry calls up Elvis's manager, Colonel Tom Parker. Jerry tells the Colonel his idea. Parker tells him no. But the word no doesn't mean no to Jerry. He keeps calling the Colonel every day—for a year. Still no dice. Then Jerry gets a call from the Colonel. The Colonel tells him if he wants to do the tour he should show up at the Hilton hotel in Las Vegas the next day with a check for a million bucks.

Of course, Jerry doesn't have the money. But he has twenty-four hours to get it. He tries everyone he knows with that kind of bankroll. No dice. Finally, at the last minute, he convinces a radio station owner in Seattle who loves Elvis to pony up. Then he goes to the nearest bank and tells the teller that he's going to need a cashier's check. It'll be for a million dollars. I wish I could have seen the teller's face.

The radio station owner from Seattle wires the money, and in a couple of hours Jerry's got this cashier's check made out to Elvis Presley. He goes to meet the Colonel. The Colonel takes the check, looks at it for a moment and then puts it in the hotel safe. That's it. The deal's done. Who needs paperwork? The Colonel takes Jerry into Elvis's suite. Elvis is easy. He's only got one request. One request. Please make sure that every seat is filled.

So Jerry has Elvis open up on the Fourth of July at the convention center. Jerry arrives in Miami Beach to find the show all sold out—all ten thousand seats. Beautiful. That gives him a better idea. How about a matinee? The box office guy eggs him on: You'll sell 20,000 seats in a single day.

The day before the show, Jerry goes back to the box office. The box office guy has a chunk of tickets in his hand. The matinee hasn't sold out. There's still five thousand empty seats in the back. Now Jerry's going crazy. What was the *one thing* Elvis told him? No empty seats.

Now Jerry's dream has turned into a nightmare. There's no time to sell five thousand tickets. What's he going to do? He goes to the arena. Looks at the seats. They're bolted to the floor. Then he walks over to the jailhouse. He asks to see the sheriff. He makes a contribution to local law enforcement in the form of a wad of cash and asks if a gang of prisoners is available to unscrew five thousand seats from the back of the arena in the morning, take them out of the building, and then screw them back in before evening.

The sheriff brings dozens of prisoners in orange jumpsuits to the convention center. The prisoners unscrew the seats, take them away to the parking lot, and cover them with a blue tarp.

Elvis does the matinee. Not an empty seat in the house. Afterward, the prisoners take all the seats back inside. They screw them in just before the evening show. It goes great. Elvis is on fire. Women are going crazy. Elvis throws his scarf into the crowd. The women are fighting for it. They're passing out. Elvis is a smash.

I wish I'd been there when Jerry took Elvis back to the hotel. I wish I'd seen the look on Jerry's face when Elvis told him, "The afternoon show went well. But it's always so much better at night."

The third moment I'd like to have seen Elvis was when he met the Beatles. It was at Elvis's hotel suite. For twenty minutes, nobody said anything. Everybody was too shy. Finally, Elvis got out his guitar. It was the Beatles doing the worshipping.

Imagine

I was doing my all-night radio show on the Mutual Broadcasting network when John Lennon was shot and killed. He was pronounced dead around 11 p.m.

I wasn't a Beatles fan at the time. I knew the Beatles were popular. But I had no idea how popular until that night. We went on the air at midnight. The phone lines were jammed with people talking about what John meant to them. People were crying. The calls came in from everywhere. From John's neighbors in New York to people on army bases all over the world. It was an extraordinary night.

I remember driving home that morning, wondering how I could have had no idea how much Lennon and the Beatles meant.

Hey Jude

I came to understand the Beatles' music through the conductor of the Boston Pops.

Arthur Fiedler said that the Beatles had produced the greatest pop music in centuries. He predicted that their songs would still be listened to in five hundred years. People had no idea of the amazing things they did with chords and arrangements, he said, and to prove it, he'd made an album of their music with the Boston Pops.

"You mean," I said, "they're gonna be Beethoven?"

"Yes," he said. Then he did a bit of "Hey Jude": *Dum, dum, dum, da-ta-da-dum. Da-ta-da-dummm. Hey Jude.* He made it classical.

She's So Fine

The first time I heard the song "My Sweet Lord," I knew. The melody had been taken from "She's So Fine." George Harrison had no idea he'd taken it. All you need to do is hit the same four notes and you've copied a song.

Something in the Way She Moves

Paul McCartney came over to my house to listen to Shawn's album. He gave her a nice critique. He played the piano. He also did a surprise performance for my producer, Wendy, at her birthday party.

When we were at the Mirage for the "Love" show, he stayed in the next suite and Ringo stayed in the suite across the way. So I ran into them in the hall a lot. We became very friendly over time.

When I was interviewing Garth Brooks, he talked about being surprised when the Beatles decided to go digital on iTunes. They'd held out for a long time, as had Garth. Garth liked the warmth of tape—and he refused to go digital. It seemed to him that the Beatles had his back. But when they went to iTunes, he felt like the only guy out there standing for what he believed. But he wasn't critical of the Beatles. He said he'd really love to talk to Paul McCartney about it.

I said, "Why not give him a call?"

Garth said he didn't feel comfortable picking up the phone to call a musical god just like that.

"Hey," I said, "I can. He played the piano in my living room."

On days like that, I go home and say to myself, *Did that really happen?*

Thriller

I met Michael Jackson a few times. But he was a very hard guy to know.

There's a story Celine Dion told me about him that painted a picture of who he was: two people.

He was in the audience one night to watch her perform. She pointed out at him and told the crowd, "Michael Jackson's here!"

He wouldn't stand up. "Michael," she said, "C'mon up on-stage and take a bow." He walked onstage all meek. The music started to play and—wow!—he starts to sing with her and he's phenomenal.

The music ends and he sits down, shy again.

The first time I met him he was about twelve years old. I interviewed the Jackson 5 in Miami on the radio. I don't re-member much—just that he was a shy, cute kid. I didn't know it at the time, but he was already reading everything he could about Walt Disney and telling his brothers that one day he was going to have a Disneyland in his backyard.

We didn't have any idea what was going on behind the scenes, how much pressure his father put on all the kids. Janet Jackson later told me how her breasts were bound when she was ten years old so she would still look like a child.

From the outside looking in, it's hard to understand what Michael was going through. We only see what we see.

I was once honored at a banquet by the Reverend Jesse Jackson. Michael was seated at my table. He was very nice, said that he watched my show. I wanted him to come on the show, so a meeting was set up to talk about it.

My friend Sid and I went to the hotel where he said he'd meet us. We waited and waited. Finally, we went into his suite and walked into a huge Batman statue. We looked around, and Michael was hiding behind the door. The same guy who was hiding behind the door was also a brilliant businessman who bought the Beatles library, cowrote "We Are the World," gave millions to charity and was charged with sexually molesting children.

I was at his memorial service. I've been to his home. I've met many members of his family. I don't think I'll ever understand all there was to Michael Jackson.

Satisfaction

I liked talking about fame with Mick Jagger. Mick told me something I never knew. He'd had some trouble over a marijuana charge about forty years before, and because of it, every time he arrives at an airport in the United States he has to go to a special room at customs in order to enter the country.

Mick said it didn't take him long to learn that drugs didn't help him as a performer. Being onstage was not a place where he wanted to feel out of control.

So many great artists have had tragic endings because of drugs: Janis Joplin. Jimmy Hendrix. Jim Morrison. Others, like Eric Clapton, managed to beat their addiction and help others through it. One thing I've never found out, in all my years of asking questions, is *Why did you start when you knew what could happen?*

Nobody has an answer. They were lonely. They were on the road. They were living a crazy lifestyle. The truth is, nobody knows.

Lenny Bruce used to say: There's got to be something good about drugs. Your life is going to be ruined and you're going to die. Let's get in line.

I was addicted to cigarettes, so I understand addiction. Even when I learned how bad it was, I didn't stop. I always felt: *It isn't going to be me.* I was like the guy who says he'll never get cancer from smoking because he only buys packs that say *May affect pregnancy.*

I told Mick something that Sinatra once told me: There's a lot to be said for longevity.

Mick said, Well, you've got no options really. Either you have longevity or you're dead.

Rudolph the Red-Nosed Reindeer

I can see my son Chance when he was younger singing it with Sting. It doesn't get better than that. Well, maybe it's a tie with seeing Chance dance with James Brown at my cardiac foundation gala.

Respect

You're talking about a legend beyond a legend when you talk about Aretha Franklin. She's won thirty-two Grammys.

When she came to sing at our cardiac foundation gala, she confirmed something I've always heard about performers. When they're doing a charity, they work harder than when they're getting paid.

But she remained the diva. She won't stay above the ninth floor in any hotel.

Cardiac Foundation Gala

Michael Bolton, Celine Dion, Rod Stewart, James Brown, Stevie Wonder, Tim McGraw, Colbie Caillat, and all the other performers who've come to my cardiac foundation gala to help raise money have given me some of the greatest moments of my life. That is, they've given me the ability to call up people who don't have the money for heart surgery and tell them that they're going to get it.

Shameless

Garth Brooks is the most genuine man I've ever met. He tells people when his T-shirts are available cheaper across the street than they are at the hotel.

When my wife was putting out an album and looking for a duet partner, I asked Garth if he would like to do a tune with Shawn.

Garth said, "I would do anything for you, but I will never, ever sing a love song with anyone but my wife."

I Dreamed a Dream

When Susan Boyle walked out on the stage of *Britain's Got Talent*, nobody expected her to sing the way she did. We never had Susan Boyles when I was young. I've never seen someone with that kind of talent come out of nowhere. It was one of the most surprising moments in television.

Volare

When I was a disc jockey I used to introduce this song as Vo-Larry. They finally wrote a song about me.

It was a huge hit for Dean Martin. I always wanted to interview Dean. But by the time the show moved out to L.A., he was really down. He'd lost his son, his firstborn. His son was a great-looking guy and an Air Force captain. On a clear day, he crashed into the same mountain near Palm Springs where Sinatra's mother's plane crashed. Dean never got over his son's death.

He used to sit alone at a restaurant on Little Santa Monica Boulevard every night. He'd order an extra plate of food and have it set at the place across from him so people wouldn't take the empty seat. He'd want to be around people, but he didn't want to talk. He'd have a bite. People would pass by, say hello, and he'd nod. Then he'd go home.

Sinatra got the idea to re-create the old days, bring the old Rat Pack out on tour. He convinced Dean to come along. They opened in Oakland and sold out. Dean was the first one onstage. He had a great line. He walked out kind of boozy with a glass in his hand and said, "How'd I do?"

But his heart wasn't in it. Two days later, he said, "Frank, I don't want to go onstage. I don't want to sing. I don't want to make people laugh."

Frank got mad at him, and Dean took Frank's private plane home. They had to bring Liza Minnelli in on short notice.

I wish I could have met Dean during the "Volare" days.

Put Your Dreams Away (For Another Day)

I don't like funerals, but Frank Sinatra had a great funeral.

I sat next to Vic Damone and Nancy Reagan. There must have been about four hundred people in the Catholic church on Bedford Drive in Beverly Hills, the Church of the Good Shepherd.

George Schlatter told funny stories. The casket was set in the middle of the aisle—not up in front of the altar. Anybody who walked in, walked by the casket. Frank's piano player was behind the curtain playing all Frank's favorites. Then, at the end, they dimmed the lights a little, put a spotlight on the casket, and played "Put Your Dreams Away (For Another Day)."

That's Life

Which brings me to the story about how I met Frank. I've told it before, but it makes me feel young, so I'm going to tell it again.

One of my mentors was Jackie Gleason. Jackie helped me

out by doing promotional spots for my shows. Once he came in for my all-night television show and rearranged the set to make it more pleasing to the viewers.

But one of the greatest things he did for me came from a simple question he posed. Jackie liked to make games out of questions. The game one night was, What in your profession is impossible?

There was a doctor with us that night. The doctor said, "In my profession, they will never make blood in a laboratory. It's impossible. You can go ten million years into the future and you'll see that blood will never be made in a lab."

Jackie looked at me and asked, "What's impossible in your profession?"

"Well," I said, "I do a local radio show every night between nine and twelve. Frank Sinatra doing my radio show for three hours on one night—that's impossible."

This was 1964. There was nobody bigger in the world than Frank Sinatra and he never did interviews. Sinatra was the only person I knew of at the time who would not return a call from the *New York Times*.

Jackie knew that Frank was performing at the Fontainebleau the next week. He asked me what night Sinatra was dark.

"Monday," I said. "He doesn't work Monday."

Jackie said, "You got him."

I said, "What are you telling me?"

He said, "You got Frank Sinatra on Monday night."

I said, "Look, if I've got Frank Sinatra on my radio show next Monday night, I've got to tell people. I've got to promote it."

"Promote it!" Jackie said.

So I went on my radio show that night and said, "Ladies

and gentlemen, next Monday night we'll have Frank Sinatra for three hours."

A station exec called me up the next day and said, "Are you kidding?"

I understood exactly where the exec was coming from. Frank had a publicity guy to make sure interviews didn't happen.

I said to the exec, "Jackie Gleason told me we'd have him."

"OK . . . ," he said, but I could tell he didn't believe it. Friday came along. The exec called. He said the station was taking out a big ad in the *Miami Herald* on Monday. A full-page ad that was going to cost a lot of money. The problem was, the business department had been calling the Fontainebleau and leaving messages to confirm that Frank would be on the show. But Frank wasn't returning the calls. The exec was more than a little nervous.

So I said, "OK, I'll call Jackie." I dialed up Jackie. "Jackie, they're nervous at the station."

Jackie said, "Are you questioning me, pal? I told you he'll be there, and he'll be there!"

"OK, Jackie," I said, "I'm sorry."

So the station runs the ad. Monday night comes. Nobody goes home. The secretaries, who worked nine to five that day, all waited. Everybody at the station stayed.

It's five minutes to nine. No Frank. No car. Nothing. It's four minutes to nine. Three minutes. Nothing. I'm supposed to go on at five after the hour. At nine o'clock sharp, a limo pulls up. Out of the car steps Frank's PR guy, Jim Mahoney. Then comes Frank. He gets up the stairs and says, "Which one's Larry King?"

Timidly, I raise my hand. "Me."

"OK," he says, "let's do it!" As we were going into the booth, the PR guy pulls me aside. He says, "I don't know how you got him. But I'll tell you one thing. He pays me big money not to do this!"

I step toward the booth and the PR guy pulls me back. "Just one thing," he says. "Don't ask about the kidnapping of his son."

So I'm thinking, better not ask about the kidnapping or Frank will walk off.

"OK," I told the PR guy. "It's none of my business."

So Frank and I go into the booth. We sit down. The light goes on. We're on the air.

Now a lot of talk-show hosts would have said, "My guest tonight is an old friend—Frank Sinatra. Great to see you again, pal."

That's bullshit. I learned a long time ago never to lie to my audience. But I just couldn't start out like this was just any other night. There was something in the air. The whole audience was wondering. Larry. Frank. Larry? Frank? It didn't make sense. Frank's on top of the world. Larry's a local radio guy making $120 a week. How does he know Frank?

I'm not going to pretend that I know him. So I'm honest. As soon as I introduce him, my first question is, "Why are you here?"

It's a good question, right? He has to tell me something. Frank appreciated the honesty.

He says, "I'll tell ya. About a month ago, just before a closing night, I got laryngitis. Couldn't sing. Couldn't speak. I didn't know what to do. We had a packed house.

"So I called up Jackie Gleason. I said, 'Jackie, will you come and do the show?'

"He said, 'OK.' So he came and did the show. It was wonderful. After the show, I walked him out to his limo, leaned in, and whispered, 'Jackie, I owe you one.'

"When I checked into the Fontainebleau Hotel there was a message to call up Jackie. So I did. I said, 'Jackie, it's Frank.' He said, 'Frank, this is the one.'"

Well, Frank and I really hit it off. Frank's a great interview. He has all the characteristics that make up a great guest: Passion. A sense of humor. Anger. And an ability to explain what you do very well.

The interview was going great, and Frank became really comfortable. I said to him, "Frank, the thing between you and the press. Has it been overplayed? Or have you been bum-rapped?"

He said, "Well, it's probably been overplayed. But I've been bum-rapped, too. Take my son's kidnapping . . ."

I look over at the PR guy and I'm thinking he's going to faint. Frank goes on to tell the whole story of the kidnapping and how the press treated him!

Why? Because he felt comfortable. Years later—after we'd done many other radio and television interviews—he wrote me a letter that included a sentence that would have made Jackie Gleason smile. It said, "What you do is you make the camera disappear."

I became very friendly with Frank as a result of that first interview. After it was over, after three hours, he said, "Hey, kid, you wanna come see the show?"

"YEAH!" I said.

"Come tomorrow night. You're sitting ringside. Bring a guest."

Now I could choose any woman in town to go see Sinatra

with me, and I knew I was going to get laid. *You wanna come see Frank Sinatra sing? We're sitting ringside!* Does it get any better than that?

I asked this pretty girl I liked, and we went to the show. We were sitting right in front of the stage having a wonderful dinner and listening to Frank Sinatra. It was great. But here's the thing. In the middle of every show, Sinatra always had a cup of tea and talked to the audience. I had no idea what was coming. All of a sudden, as he's drinking his cup of tea, he says, "By the way, I don't do interviews. But I want to tell you about a young man in the audience tonight. I owed a favor to Jackie Gleason, and Jackie introduced me to this guy, and I did an interview with him, and he was terrific. It was a great interview. I want him to take a bow. You're going to be hearing a lot about him. Larry King, stand up."

Now, the girl and I are in the middle of dessert. I'm eating cherries jubilee. I have no idea that Frank is going to introduce me. In my haste to stand, I bump the table, the cherries jubilee goes flying and lands all over my white shirt and pants. There's nowhere to hide. Cherries jubilee is very red. Sinatra starts to laugh. The band is laughing. The audience is laughing. The girl is laughing.

It's really embarrassing. But what can I do? I wipe myself off, and we enjoy the second half of the show.

The performance ends and it's time to drive the girl home. I know it's going to be a good night. But after paying the bill, I have, like, eighteen dollars left in my pocket. I know I need three dollars for the car. So I leave fifteen dollars as a tip for the waiter. When I give the valet three dollars for the car, I have absolutely nothing left. But that's OK. The girl has already invited me home.

On the way, she says, "Oh, I don't have any coffee. Why don't we stop and bring home a couple of containers?"

What am I going to do with this dilemma? I'm a big shot who just took her to see Frank Sinatra and I don't have a cent in my pocket.

So I pull into a Royal Castle. I tell her to wait in the car, that I'll be right back. A few minutes later I come back to the car without anything.

She says, "Where's the coffee?"

I say, "They can't change a hundred dollar bill."

Baby

My wife is always telling me to stop talking about Sinatra when I'm asked about music. I get her point. Stay current. Hey, I met Justin Bieber at the White House Correspondents' Dinner. I've had dinner with Justin Timberlake. I met the Jonas Brothers when we did a show at the new stadium in Dallas.

The thing is, when I met the Jonas Brothers, my name was running across the stadium's scoreboard in letters fifty feet high. So it was different from when I had no money and wished I could get in to see Sinatra at the Paramount. Plus, I don't have any stories about Justin Bieber and a pie fight. So I'm going to tell one more about Frank.

The Way You Look Tonight

Frank was a complicated guy. Complicated because he was not the brightest guy in the world, but in some areas, was extraordinarily intelligent. His lyrical interpretations were genius, but he was also right out of the streets of Hoboken. He took everything personally. He was a big-deal Democrat, but when Kennedy crossed him, he became a Republican. Sometimes you could cross him and not even know it. This story is a good example.

Frank had finished a show in Miami Beach. This was back in the early sixties. He didn't like to sleep and he headed over to the coffee shop at the Fontainebleau at four in the morning. Three pals were with him. They talked over coffee for a while, and then Frank decided he wanted a piece of cherry pie.

He looked around for the waitress. No waitress. She was in the bathroom. So Frank walked over to the counter. There was a cherry pie in one of those clear pie displays—the kind that has a tray and a removable top to keep the pie fresh. Right in front of the pie holder was a guy sitting at the counter.

Frank leaned across the guy, took the top off, and got the cherry pie. Realizing he'd brushed into the guy, he said, "I'm sorry."

"Get your hands off my shoulder," the guy said.

This was not the wisest response. The word was out that Frank was connected to the highest levels of the Mob. I once asked Don Rickles, "Supposing Frank asked me to do something and I didn't want to do it?" Don said, "You got relatives still living?"

The guy couldn't have mistaken Frank for anybody else. There was no bigger entertainer in the world at the time. Frank looked him up and down. "What did you say?"

"There's nobody else at the counter," the guy said. You didn't have to lean over my shoulder to get to the pie. Keep your hands off me."

Sinatra picked up the cherry pie and hit the guy in the face with it.

The guy slowly wiped it off. Then he reached for an apple pie and hit Frank in the face with it.

The three guys at Frank's table see this and very swiftly begin to make their way over. Only it doesn't turn out like you'd think. Frank gets mad that his guys are interfering. *Why is this any of your business?* And he turns on his buddies. He and the guy at the counter *team up* and start smashing pies into the faces of Frank's friends.

The six of them got to every pie in the place and destroyed the entire coffee shop. Front-page pictures of the wreckage ended up all over the *Miami Herald*. They couldn't reopen until late the next morning.

With Frank you never knew.

As long as we can remember the music, we will always be able to be young again. And if it seems like this chapter is going on and on, you're right. That's because I don't want it to end.

5

Movies

I'm often asked who's been my favorite interview. There's just no answer to that. I'm proud of so many of them.

But a guy recently came at me from a different angle. What's the one interview, he wanted to know, that I'm most asked about?

It ain't even close. The one where Marlon Brando kissed me on the lips.

We were comparing that interview to the one I did with Al Pacino that aired as the show began its final two weeks. Then the guy asked, Would you be happy if the only work you'd left behind were your interviews with Brando and Pacino?

No, I wouldn't. What's important to me is my body of work. But I understand where his question was coming from. It was really about legacy. How would I like to be remembered?

My favorite way would probably be: *Larry King. One hundred and eight years old and still going strong . . .* But I think George Bush 43 had the best response to the legacy question. That is: "I'm not going to be here, so why worry about it?"

The guy who asked about Brando and Pacino does make a good point. The interviews with those two actors will live on long after I'm gone. I doubt that many people are going to look back to see me ask Congresswoman Michelle Bachman about her views on immigration in the early part of the twenty-first century. But a hundred years from now, when people watch *The Godfather* and want to know about the actors, they'll be able to find out through the archive of *Larry King Live*. So I know I've left a mark. There aren't many places where you can find Al Pacino sitting for an hour and talking about what he does.

Jay Leno told me it drove him nuts to watch my interviews with Brando and Elizabeth Taylor because his show always tried to book them and could never get them. There's a reason that Pacino doesn't do many interviews. Al doesn't like to be seen on screen as himself. That way, it's easier for the audience to suspend its disbelief when it sees him as Jack Kevorkian.

It took me years to convince Al to come on my show—and he's a friend of mine! When I say friend, I don't use the word lightly. He was best man at my wedding to Shawn.

I think the reason he came on as my show approached its close was out of respect for my body of work. We taped it in his backyard and held it for the last couple of weeks of the show because we wanted to go out with the greats. It was one of those interviews you didn't want to end—like when I sat down with Nelson Mandela. But at the same time it was difficult. It was hard because, for me, friends are the toughest people to interview. You know too much. You've got to search for new areas. If I ask questions that I already know the answer to, then *I'm* acting.

It wasn't easy for Al, either. His girlfriend told me he was anxious the whole week leading up to it. Al is a quirky guy. If

I'm going to see him perform on Broadway, he'll want to make sure I have a ticket, but he won't want to know what night I'm in the theater.

My friendship with Al is easy to understand. We both came up poor, as street kids. Me in Brooklyn, Al in the Bronx. But Al is much more complicated than me. He's been living inside many people. He's been Jack Kevorkian and Frank Serpico. That's different from acting out Shakespeare. He's had to turn himself into people who are alive, people who'd be watching him. And when he is acting Shakespeare, he has to choose which of the many different ways to play his role. I remember Charlton Heston telling me there are ten ways you could play Hamlet—from brave to psychotic. Me, I just show up on time and ask questions that pop into my mind. Al is constantly searching for ways to get inside these personalities.

Brando once did some sessions at the University of Southern California in which he called acting "Lying for a Living." "Isn't that a good description?" I once asked Al. "Absolutely not," he shot back. "I'm not lying at all. That's who I am. I'm Al Pacino, but I'm also Shylock. I *am* Shylock." Al thought the better the actor, the more truth you see, because the actor is letting himself out. The irony is, nobody let himself out better than Brando.

Maybe the difference between Marlon and Al was that it came easy to Brando. Al has to work at it. People who have to work harder are amazed at people who don't.

I've talked to so many actors over the years and heard so many different approaches. I guess that's why they make such a unique breed. You couldn't find two guys who go about their work more differently than Clint Eastwood and Warren Beatty. Clint is a minimalist. What you see is what you get. He's that way when you have dinner with him. He's serious—the same

95

way he acts and directs. He wants to do the take and move on. Which is the exact opposite of Warren Beatty. Warren is: Let's try this. Let's try that. Soon, it's: *Take 68!*

Then you had the sharp differences between old school and new. I remember talking to Franchot Tone, a wonderful actor out of the studio system who starred in *Mutiny on the Bounty* back in the thirties. Tone told me he never varied from the script. Whatever the script said, that was the way he acted. I asked him, "What if a fly landed on your nose during filming?" He said, "I would not brush it away, because brushing it away is not on the page."

Anthony Quinn couldn't have been more different. As Jackie Gleason once told me: "Anthony Quinn doesn't act—he marinates." When they were doing *Requiem for a Heavyweight*, Quinn played the fighter and Jackie the manager. A scene came up that was supposed to take place after Quinn had just finished a long fight. Quinn didn't feel up to filming it because he was too fresh. "Give me fifteen minutes," he said. He ran around the block a few times, then came back winded and ready.

Quinn couldn't fathom the old-school guys. He was absolutely astonished by Laurence Olivier on the opening night of *Becket*. The rehearsals had gone well, but they were only rehearsals. Now it was opening night. Quinn was playing King Henry. He had totally become the King. He was the King onstage. He was the King offstage. He was the King at home. He was sitting on the throne for the opening performance. Olivier was standing next to him. The Queen was speaking. There was a tension throughout the house. Olivier leans over to him. Olivier is not supposed to say anything. But he whispers: "Where do you get a really good beer in New York?"

Quinn watched the final scene from behind the curtain in disbelief. Olivier was giving the death speech. A spear was in him. The curtain came down. The audience was applauding. And Olivier says, "Move the blue light."

Olivier got as much respect as Brando, because he was able to bring powerful emotions to the stage without having to live them.

Dustin Hoffman was at the other polar extreme from Olivier. I remember meeting Dustin while he was filming *Midnight Cowboy*. I was invited to the set in Florida see some of the scenes being shot where Ratso Rizzo dies on the bus. Dustin had me over for lunch at his hotel. He was seated, but then he said, "Let me lower the blinds." He walked to the blinds with Ratso's limp.

"Why are you doing that?" I asked.

"Oh, I've been doing this for two months," he said. "I don't want to forget the limp."

Olivier would say, *Just limp!*

Yet they all figured out a way to get to the same place on-screen—that seamless place where the audience doesn't get a sense of the actor's effort.

It must be doubly hard to get to that place when you're very attractive. Elizabeth Taylor was a damn good actress who was so beautiful that people couldn't fully appreciate her talents. You were mesmerized by those purple eyes, those magnificent breasts. Yeah, she won two Academy Awards. But when you watched her play Cleopatra, it was nearly impossible to forget who you were looking at. Meryl Streep doesn't have that kind of beauty, and it's a benefit. I just saw a picture of her in makeup dressed as Margaret Thatcher. It was unbelievable. She could be a double.

Think of how hard it is for Brad Pitt and George Clooney to get your wife or girlfriend to suspend disbelief. I mean, if your wife ran off with George Clooney, how could you even be mad? One time I was hosting a charity event. George, Shawn and I were together, arms interlocked, when someone called me over. I started to walk off and Shawn said, "Don't hurry back!"

That was one of the things that made Brando so remarkable. He was handsome, dynamic. But his looks didn't get in the way when he played a bastard in *Streetcar Named Desire*. As Sidney Poitier once told me, when you watched Brando on stage you didn't think you were in a theater. Brando made you think you were peeking in on someone's life. It's hard to imagine what Brando must have meant to other actors at that time, to see a guy do what many of them didn't know was possible.

Pacino was mesmerized when he saw Brando in *On the Waterfront*. Al was about sixteen. He went into a movie house for a double feature. The first film was *A Member of the Wedding*. Great movie. Then *On the Waterfront* comes on, and Al is just locked in. He's never seen anything like it. The movie ends and he doesn't move. He stays in his seat and sits through *A Member of the Wedding* again just to see *On the Waterfront* a second time.

I can still remember that scene where Marlon's walking with Eva Marie Saint in the park. She drops her glove, and he picks it up, then puts it on his own hand. What a great moment. Here's this tough longshoreman bonding with this young girl over this petite glove. Plus, the sexual innuendo. The dropped glove was not in the script. Marlon took an accident and turned it into a moment that you remember more than half a century later.

There was another free-flowing moment that gets at the essence of Brando. It happened during *The Godfather*—right before the Don dies running around the tomato vines. Just before, he's giving advice to his son Michael. Do this. Do that. A server comes by. Would you like some wine? They're both supposed to wave him off. The server is interrupting an important conversation. But Marlon says, "I like to drink wine more than I used to." Al had no idea it was coming. It wasn't in the script. But the nuance said it all: The Don was at the end of the road.

Maybe it came *too* easy to Brando. There were actors who felt that he wasn't respectful. Rod Steiger, to his death, resented Marlon because of that famous scene in *On the Waterfront*— the scene Marlon made famous with the line: "I could've been a contender." Steiger sat next to Marlon in the back of the car when Marlon did his lines. But Marlon wasn't there for Steiger's. *Hey, I fed him his lines. Why didn't he feed me mine?*

Elizabeth Taylor told me that she loved working with Marlon, but was put off by his lack of preparation. He'd forget his lines—*Oops, sorry. Can we do another take? Oops, sorry, can we do another?* He'd just play it that way until he was happy. In *Last Tango in Paris*, he had his lines written on a wall that he could see off camera while he was having sex with Maria Schneider. And he put on so much weight over time that he looked like he was four hundred pounds. You couldn't help but wonder: How'd he let himself go?

It got to the point where many believed that he'd turned on his profession. He'd say things like, "I don't have to play Shakespeare. I can read him. Why do I have to stand onstage and emote it? Just read it. The guy was a great writer." Actors were pissed at that. When *Apocalypse Now* came out, it was widely discussed on college campuses. Martin Sheen had a heart attack during the making of it. Brando was a crazy character—Colonel Kurtz. Pauline Kael analyzed the film in a big essay for *The New Yorker*. It wasn't a commercial success, but everyone was talking about it. When an interviewer approached Brando and asked about *Apocalypse Now*, Marlon replied, "Is that the one where I was bald?"

One moment, he could be a jester. The next, he could be making a heartfelt political stand. He couldn't be intimidated. Yet he moved to Tahiti partly as an escape from fame. He knew he was being stared at. But he never seemed self-conscious about all the weight he carried around.

So you had no idea what was coming when you interviewed Brando. He did things his way, and he did them instinctively, and in the moment—which is pretty well how my meeting with him came about.

Brando wasn't doing interviews in 1994. But he'd been paid $5 million to write his autobiography, and he found out that if he didn't do a television interview to promote it he'd be in breach of contract. So he called up and said he was going to send a car over to bring me to his house. The next thing you know he's pulling up to meet me in a white Chevrolet. The doorman at CNN couldn't believe it. Soon, we were singing through the streets.

The interview was set to take place at his home a couple of days later. My staffers arrived early to work on the lighting. There's nothing in his home that gives any hint that he's an actor. I don't even think Marlon knew where his Academy Awards were. So the crew is setting up and he comes out of his bedroom in a T-shirt that doesn't quite fit and his underwear. It's become clear over time that my producer on set, Carrie Stevenson, will never forget that moment.

But that was the essence of Marlon. His very entrance into the room created drama. During the interview Marlon said that unless we look inward we won't ever be able to clearly see outward. I've never been one to get too psychological. But if the reverse applies, the interview is a glimpse at the inner Brando. Marlon came on the show in a jacket that a guy working in a service station might wear, and a tie, but no socks or shoes—

a fact he quickly pointed out. He tried to turn the tables and interview me. When he didn't like a question he diverted it by softly slapping my face in an affectionate way. He warned of global warming. He beckoned his 150-pound mastiff onto the set and then asked me to feed it a treat mouth-to-mouth. Never, in all my years of interviewing, has a guest caught me looking at my watch and asked me why I was doing so—only Marlon. He noticed everything around him and used it for his own purposes. So many other guests would have refrained from commenting on the sweat that broke out on my face under the harsh lights. Not Marlon. "Get this guy a Kleenex!"

It all came naturally to him. I think it explains why Brando didn't elevate acting to some exalted terrain. He said that acting was older than humanity. The drunk in the bar who threatens to attack you—"What are you looking at?"—Brando compared to the silverback gorilla that doesn't like it when you get too close. Marlon was just doing what we all do everyday—acting. Only he made it an art form. At the end of the hour, we sang a song and he kissed me on the lips.

I'm often asked what it was like to be kissed on the lips by Marlon Brando. "I can't stop thinking about it," is the best I can do—because it's the truth. I couldn't stop looking at him when I was around him and I couldn't stop remembering the experience afterward—I think he had that affect on everyone. And I can't stop talking about it, because sixteen years later people are still asking. There is another memory from that day. I can picture Marlon walking around after the interview, serving the crew champagne. He didn't want anybody to leave.

We did another interview some years later. Afterward, I was with Marlon and several women when one of them asked if he could dance. In fact, his mother was a dancer, and he'd gone to New York as a young man in the hopes of becoming a dancer. There was tension as Marlon stepped forward and reached for this woman's hand. You didn't know how it was going to go because of his enormous weight. But he was so light on his feet. He just waltzed her around the room. You never saw the heaviness. Everything he did was infused with drama. Drama was like breathing to Marlon.

If you went out to eat with him at a restaurant, he'd point around the room and reveal deep secrets.

"See that couple over there? They don't have another six months together. Look at the way he crosses his leg. Look at his eye, it's going right over her left shoulder. No chance."

"Look at the way the maître d' turns after he shows someone to the table. He's unhappy."

Marlon didn't order anything for himself. He ate off everybody else's plate. He gave me a pass code to reach him on the phone. I'd dial his number. When he'd answer, I'd have to say, "The ship is in." That was my code.

Then he'd say, "Hello, Larry."

After that second interview, he called me in the middle of the night.

"C'mon, we're going to Mexico."

"Marlon, it's two in the morning."

"I'll meet you at Van Nuys."

I started to get dressed. He called me back. The trip was off. Sean Penn couldn't find his passport.

The more I got to know him, the wilder things got. He once proposed we do an interview in Tahiti, with a camera overlooking us as we both lay naked on a roof.

Sometimes when you live your life doing something all the time, you end up being it. That was Marlon. He told me if twice a year people left $5 million on his doorstep he'd never act again. I don't doubt it—because there was enough drama in his life.

FRANK SINATRA

May 31, 1988

Dear Larry,

I've been on the road since we were
together, but I do want to steal a
minute now to tell you how much I
enjoyed being with you recently.
Even without the cameras and the mikes
it would have been a pleasure.

Since the broadcast, we have received
all kinds of communications about
the appearance with you. Calls from
friends, mail from strangers and
friends and hello's from both.
All seemed to have enjoyed our joint
appearance and were quite enthusiastic
about both of us. You should know
what an audience you have out there -
with or without a guest. As one guy
put it: "Larry's the best. I wouldn't
miss him".

In all honesty I was never worried
about how it would go. You are a good
friend and - unlike so many others -
were not there to trap or ensnare me
or to sensationalize in any way. I
enjoyed every minute of it and felt,
as I always do, completely comfortable
with you.

Be aware, my friend, you are very rare
in your line of work, never asking self
serving questions or competing with
your guests in any way. And you'll
never know how much that means to all
of us who have sat opposite you.

I am deeply indebted, and I hope one
day soon we can take another crack at
it.

With my deep appreciation and warmest
regards,

Francis Albert

The letter that Frank Sinatra sent me in 1988 is one of my most
cherished treasures. You can tell it's from Frank because he
always signed his letters with his full first name.

I was surprised to find out how much in common I have
with the world's richest man, Carlos Slim.

(Credit: Simon Cordova. Courtesy of Larry King.)

The interview I'm most asked about is the one in which
I was kissed by Marlon Brando.

It took years of coaxing, but my good friend and best man, Al Pacino,
finally came on the show just before *Larry King Live* ended
after twenty-five years.

No subject I interviewed during the last year of the show got more
reaction on the street than did Mahmoud Ahmadinejad.

One of my proudest accomplishments of the last year was
raising $9 million for the earthquake victims of Haiti—
with help from Seal and a lot of others.

I had no idea who would appear on the final show. Bill Maher
and Ryan Seacrest were the perfect guest-hosts.

Conan O'Brien spent half a year off the air after his departure
from NBC. After I announced I was leaving my cable show,
he joked, "I'm always here for advice."

My producer Wendy Walker may be the most organized person in the world. She added just the right touch at the postfinale celebration.

My staff, who made it all happen. All I did was show up,
put on my suspenders and ask questions.

Now, Al, I don't think he'd ever say that. Al comes out to California and shoots two weeks of a comedy and then flies back to New York in the morning and becomes Shylock on Broadway later that night. If you ask Al to respond to a film clip, he'll study it carefully before he says a word. Marlon wouldn't even look at the clip.

No interview was quite like Brando's. But that's also what made it great to come into work whenever an actor was a guest. The interviews could be as different as their approaches. Plus, you never knew if they were acting. How could you? They're trained as actors. But even if they were acting, they were revealing themselves in their own way.

Sidney Poitier could be analytical about the craft. Paul Newman would rather talk about salad dressing.

Tom Hanks would beam at a compliment. He lit up when I told him how highly Jackie Gleason thought of him in *Nothing in Common*. Bette Davis couldn't care less if she hurt anybody's feelings. "What's it like to work with Faye Dunaway?" I once asked her. "I'd prefer," she replied, "to work with professionals."

Lauren Bacall was honest enough to discuss how unhappy she was with Frank Sinatra, who swept her off her feet after Humphrey Bogart's death, proposed, and then took off. But asking Angelina Jolie about her difficult relationship with her father was like running into a brick wall.

Tom Cruise was game for a swordfight to kick off the release of *The Last Samurai*. Robert De Niro's hesitations and short responses made you realize that his movies are his form of self-expression.

James Caan is a cutup. Robert Duvall said that it was much more fun to make *Godfather* than *Godfather II* because Caan was in the first. Sean Penn is intense. Don't ask him a question about acting if you have him on a show about aiding Haiti after the earthquake.

Hilary Swank arrived more beautiful in person than she is on-screen. Charlton Heston complained that his looks were unfair. "I can't be the guy down the street," he said. "I've got to play Moses." Then there was the advice Mel Brooks gave Frank Langella when they did *The Twelve Chairs*. "Frank, you could be a star but you're too good looking. So my suggestion for your career is to run across the room, and I slam a door into your face. Then, don't change a thing."

Daniel Day-Lewis had a reputation for being aloof, but he came in like an old friend. I so looked forward to interviewing Robert Mitchum—until he refused to answer my questions. For an entire hour he one-worded me. His son later told me that he was probably putting me on.

Sylvester Stallone could inspire you with the story of how he refused to let go of Rocky even when the studios offered big money to take his script if the actor in him would step aside. Jack Lemmon could make you laugh as he smacked himself for turning down one of the lead roles in *The Hustler*. *A movie about pool? Who's gonna watch a movie about pool?* When he attended the premiere, he jumped up and screamed: "I fucked up again!"

Yul Brynner would happily explain why he would work only if his lodgings came with brown wallpaper and Hungarian goat milk. Albert Brooks would happily explain the difference between the old theater experience and the new. He did it like this, as only Albert Brooks could: "Forty years ago Mabel and Isabel are standing in line in Des Moines for the new John Wayne movie. Mabel says, 'I hear it's wonderful. The girl is terrific. There's a lot of fighting and some tender scenes. It's a real good movie. You get your free plate.' The same two people now:

Mabel says, 'You know, it cost $80 million. I don't know if they can recoup. Maybe if they sell it to HBO. If not, they've got to get a foreign deal . . .'"

So many Oscar winners talked about how much the award meant to them. George C. Scott straightaway explained why he didn't accept his for *Patton*. The only way to judge performances, he said, is five men playing the same role directed by the same person. Made sense to me.

I could go on all day. Gene Hackman. Audrey Hepburn. Jason Robards. Julia Roberts. Kirk Douglas. Michael Douglas. Diane Keaton. Jeff Bridges. Nicole Kidman. Peter O'Toole. Jodie Foster. Richard Dreyfuss. Shirley MacLaine. Denzel Washington. But there was no better closer than Al.

Al, who doesn't like to be interviewed because he's basically shy. Al, who likes to be interviewed because he's got a big personality underneath the shyness. Al, who is cerebral and loves to talk about the craft. Al, who through it all has never lost the freshness and spirit of a street kid.

There's a story I love that goes back to one of the first plays he was in. The production had a crowd scene. In this scene, a bomb went off. Al's part called for him to yell, "That sounds like a bomb!"

He rehearsed the line all week.

"That sounds like a bomb!"

"That sounds like a bomb!"

"That sounds like a bomb!"

They never set the bomb off during rehearsal. They just told him that the sound would come on opening night.

On opening night, the scene arrived, and the bomb went off. BOOM!

And Al said, "What the fuck was that?"

I found myself just as amused years later when Jerry

Weintraub told me about getting Al ready for the filming of *Ocean's Thirteen*. Al was playing a hotel manager and he had to look sharp. So Weintraub sent him to Las Vegas to spend a week with hotel managers to get the flavor. Then Jerry said, "You've got to get a manicure."

"Why?" Al wanted to know.

"Because these hotel managers get manicures all the time."

Al went to get the manicure. The manicurist called Jerry and said, "This is not a manicure. This is surgery. This man hasn't had a manicure in thirty years."

Jerry said, "I'll tell you what. Give him a pedicure, too."

So now Al has to get a pedicure. Al calls up Jerry and says: "Are there scenes in this movie where I'm barefoot?"

"No," Jerry says. "But I just wanted to give you the feeling."

He comes in for the shoot and tells Jerry, "The girl scratched me under the cuticles, and I kicked her in the head."

I know exactly what he means. The woman who gives me my pedicures touches the soles of my feet at her peril.

Now, Marlon wouldn't allow you to ask where the essence of his character in *The Godfather* came from. But Al would. So it was fun to look back.

I remember sitting in the balcony of a mobbed theater when *The Godfather* came out. I'd read the book, so I was somewhat prepared. But when I walked out of that theater, I knew this was something special. What I didn't know was that Al had almost lost his role.

He recalled how sensitive Marlon was to him, because everyone on the set seemed to sense he was going to lose the job. Al had started off playing Michael a bit erratically. It makes sense: Michael had just come out of the Army; he wasn't a gangster. He was forced into it over time. Everything just kind of happens to him. Al thought if he played him as the guy who was going to take over from the get-go, there'd be nowhere to go. There'd be no space for that moment of change. So he approached Michael as an independent guy, but a kid who doesn't know who he really is. The problem was, the director couldn't see who Michael really was either. Finally, Francis Ford Coppola called him in and said, "You're not cutting it for me, kid." Coppola had Al sit and watch some of the rushes. By that time, Al didn't even want to be in the movie anymore. *Hey, if you don't want me . . .*

But the rushes told him exactly what Coppola was talking about. "You know, what?" Al said. "You're right." He knew he was onto something. It was just off the mark.

The next scene they shot was the one where he gets the gun from the bathroom and kills the two guys in the restaurant in revenge for the shooting of his father. He went into it thinking that it might be his last scene. And *that's* the scene where he discovers Michael Corleone. The look in his eyes as he drops the gun will live for as long as people can talk about it.

Al spoke about learning to be blind for *Scent of a Woman* from his three-year-old daughter. He asked her how to do a blind person, and she was spot on. No preparation. *Bam!* So Al did a variation on her theme. He got to the point where by not focusing his eyes, he actually wasn't seeing, and then he injured himself when he fell into a bush and a branch scratched his cornea.

It was exploration, then discovery. The phrase *huah!* came to him when he was learning how to assemble and disassemble a .45 while acting blind. He spent countless hours working on it and when he finally nailed it, the military instructor let out a *huah!* There it was.

Other times it was the reverse. Self-discovery led to exploration. He had to understand what was happening to his life before he could accept his role in *Dog Day Afternoon*. He was drinking too much at the time and he turned down the script after initially accepting it. One of the producers had to implore him to stop drinking for a few days so he could read the script again with a clear head. Al didn't drink for a few days, read it and said, "Why am I not doing this?"

During the shooting, a guy came over to Al and wondered if he might want to spice up the dialogue by referencing the prison uprising that had just shaken New York State. Now we'll never forget the word *Attica!*

"Say hello to my little friend," in *Scarface*, came from his little son.

We could have spent all day talking about acting and all night talking about the Yankees. But it's a show, and soon it was over.

When I walked away from the interview, the same guy who asked me the legacy question wanted to know what it felt like. After 50,000 interviews, he asked, did it feel good to know that I could do what I do as well at seventy-seven as I ever could?

The question reminded me of an interview I once did with the golfer Sam Snead. Sammy had a perfect swing. The world has never seen a swing like Sam Snead's. Slammin' Sammy Snead. I said to Sammy, "You're seventy now. Could you play in a tournament?" He said, "I could probably play on Thursday. But then Friday would be hard. But I'll tell you what. I'll play any player in the world one hole for money— and they can pick the hole." I never forgot that. *And they can pick the hole.*

My point is: I'm not Sam Snead. I didn't feel like, *And they can pick the hole.* I didn't feel like that because the interview wasn't about me. Al Pacino hit the home run that day. Not me. I was the facilitator. That's the job. To get the guest to open up so he or she can hit a home run. That's what a lot of people in broadcasting don't understand these days. But we'll get to that later on . . .

6

Crime

This is a serious topic. So let me ease into it with a funny story. The topic is crime. The story goes back to when I was just making a name for myself as a radio show host in Miami.

There was a convention for police chiefs and another for district attorneys taking place over the same few days. They were both ending with Sunday afternoon sessions. Somebody came up with the idea to cancel both afternoon sessions, rent out the ballroom at the Fontainebleau Hotel on Sunday night, and conclude both conventions with a combined dinner.

This created a slight problem. The problem being that the most boring man on the planet was scheduled to speak to the district attorneys. The change would put him in front of the combined audience at the finale. So my friend, the state attorney in Miami, asked me for a favor: Will you please follow this guy and save the evening?

"I'm just a local radio guy," I said. "Nobody knows me."

"Don't worry," he said. "I'll give you a big introduction."

So I go there Sunday night. I'm seated on the dais next to police chiefs from around America—all in uniform. I'm a little overwhelmed. My friend the state attorney comes over and says, "Relax. No problem."

Then, Frank Silverman gets up to speak. It's hard to make the subject of crime boring, but Frank Silverman turned it into a commercial for Sominex. His own wife went face-first into the Baked Alaska. Frank droned on and on about how to solve crime. As soon as he stopped, half the crowd miraculously awakened and started running for the door.

My friend the state attorney went to the microphone and said, "Now, before you leave, here's my friend—Larry King."

That was my big introduction.

So I rushed to the microphone and screamed, "Hold it! Wait a minute!

The crowd turned.

"I'm in broadcasting! Yes, broadcasting! In broadcasting we have an equal time code! A fairness doctrine! You have just heard Frank Silverman speak against crime. I'm here to speak *on behalf* of crime."

It's a cliché to say you could have heard a pin drop. Believe me, at that moment you could have heard the tinkle. Everybody sat down. *I've got them*, I thought. Only now, I have to think of something to say.

"How many people in this room," I ask, "would like to live in Butte, Montana?"

Nobody raises a hand.

I slammed the lectern. "You see! Nobody wants to live in Butte, Montana! Butte, Montana, is the city with the lowest crime rate in the Western world! Last year, there were no crimes in Butte! There is not even a locksmith in Butte, Montana!

"Tell me, what are the top five crime cities in America? New York, Chicago, Las Vegas, Los Angeles, and Miami—the top five tourist cities. So you see, crime is a major tourist attraction. You put crime in your community, you're gonna double the size of the airport. People flock to crime.

"And another thing that *he*"—I'm pointing at the suddenly important Frank Silverman—"didn't mention. The money stays local. The local bookmaker goes to the local coffee shop. The local hooker goes to the local beauty parlor.

"And! Criminals have a tendency to take care of their own problems. They don't put added stress on the police department. They commit crimes you don't have to solve.

"One more thing that Frank Silverman totally left out. If we listen to everything he says, and we do everything he wants us to do, we will wipe out crime in America. Think of the consequences. The unemployment rate in this room is going to hit 100 percent!"

From the middle of the crowd, the police chief from Louisville jumped up and said, "What can we do to help?"

I bring up that story to make a larger point. There's always more than one way to see a crime. Crime is rarely simple—and it's very often complex. It can also put innocent bystanders in no-win situations. Like the time Bob Costas was eating dinner in a restaurant and found out that the mobster John Gotti had picked up his check for him. Do you go over and shake his hand? Or do you refuse the offer? Is there a diplomatic way out? Crime can even make us wonder about our own sense of values. Like the time Yogi Berra was asked what he'd do if he stumbled upon a million dollars in the street while nobody was looking. "I'd find the guy who lost it," Yogi said. "And if he was poor, I'd give it back."

Bottom line is, crime is very rarely black and white.

Wesley Snipes was the guest the night after the Al Pacino interview aired. I thought he was terrific with Halle Berry in *Flight 57*, but he wasn't on to discuss an upcoming film. He came on as a man about to surrender himself to a federal prison in less than forty-eight hours.

It was a very confusing story. Ultimately, he was convicted of three misdemeanor counts of failing to file federal tax returns in 1999, 2000, and 2001.

Snipes claimed he was innocent. He claimed that someone else was supposed to file the taxes for him. The jury agreed in part—acquitting him of two felony charges. The judge gave him the max: three years in prison.

Wesley was hoping my show would allow people to see his case in a different light and halt his incarceration. One of his big problems was that the case had attracted the attention of groups that believe *nobody* should have to pay taxes. He became a poster child for these groups. So it was plausible that the government wanted to make an example of him. Wesley's attorney said he'd paid more than $30 million in taxes and that he'd shown up in court with a $6 million check to try to resolve the problem. You couldn't help but wonder. Why was that check rejected? Wouldn't anyone want to look into the case after it came to light that the chief witness against him turned out to be the same business manager who'd ripped off Al Pacino for millions? But also, why did Wesley wait until the last minute to make his case public?

It was hard to do the story justice. To do it right you needed to have the prosecutor on the show. Anyone can look like they were railroaded in a case when you don't hear from the other side.

Which is why I'd really like to interview Bernie Madoff.

Because when it comes to Bernie Madoff, there doesn't seem to be another side. If there is, I'd like to hear it.

I'm often asked to name someone I would have liked to interview but never got the chance. Near the top of the list would have to be Madoff. There would be a double lure—it would be a victim interview. I've never interviewed anybody who ever committed a crime against me.

I was one of thousands of "investors" who got taken by Madoff. *Time* magazine estimates there were up to 3 million direct and indirect victims. In some ways, you could say I'm the last guy who should have fallen for his scheme. Over the years, I've talked with FBI agents about great frauds and Secret Service agents about counterfeiting. I've sat down with the legendary bank robber Willie Sutton. Recalling great crime capers always makes for a great breakfast at Nate 'n Al's. After hearing all those stories, how could a guy like me not have a clue?

There's a good answer to that. Bernie Madoff was brilliant. There was even a little Willie Sutton in him. Willie was a robber, but he never carried a gun. He had an amazing mind and he had that great line. I said to him, "You could have been a giant of industry. Why rob banks?"

"That's where the money is."

It was logical to him. He was more interested in being outside the law than inside. Robbery attracted his cunning.

Once Sutton pulled off a bank robbery in Queens. Get this setup: What Willie did was go to the bank for months in various disguises—a couple of them female. He opened about eight accounts, deposited money, made withdrawals. The idea was to go almost every day so that all the tellers trusted his

115

characters. In a sense, he befriended the people at the bank. All the while, he was casing the joint.

It took him a couple of months to know every move. He knew exactly when the Brinks boys made their pickups. Then, one day at precisely that time, he came in dressed as a pregnant woman. That gave him ample room to hide bags filled with confetti next to his stomach. The bags looked just like the ones the bank used for the Brinks pickups. He casually switched his bags for ones that had cash and walked out the door. There were no video cameras in those days to replay what had happened. Nobody even discovered the switch until that night when the money was counted.

You know how cunning Willie was? He kept going back to the bank dressed in the different disguises for weeks after the robbery. The investigators never suspected any of his characters because none of them stopped making deposits. The police just couldn't solve the crime. They found out only when Sutton was caught for another robbery and decided to confess.

One reason why Madoff's scheme worked for as long as it did was that he was disguised. He didn't need a costume as elaborate as maternity wear. His disguise was much better than that. He was disguised as himself—the former chairman of NASDAQ and a pillar of the Jewish community. Charities trusted him to watch over their money—and, why not, he made large donations. Who would rip off a charity? What Jew would rip off Elie Wiesel—a Holocaust survivor? Madoff was the best friend of respected and well-known people. Is there a better way to lure in someone than with a friend's recommendation?

Shawn once mentioned to Freddie Wilpon that we were looking for investment advice, and Freddie said, "Ever hear of Bernie Madoff? He's been my friend for years . . ."

Freddie is the owner of the New York Mets. Freddie has been *my* friend for years. Of course I'm going to listen when he says, "Madoff's the best. The best! I'll try to get you in with him. I'll try . . ."

This was yet another lure Madoff had going for him— exclusivity. Madoff didn't take just anybody. So there wasn't a normal vetting process. Instead, Madoff had *me* wondering if my money was good enough for him to handle. When Freddie called back and said, "Good news! Madoff will take you," I wasn't thinking about checking the guy out. I was happy to be accepted into the club.

I spoke with my accountants. No warning bells there. They never even spoke to Madoff. They talked with one of his guys. We sent him $250,000 to start. A month later, we got a list of stocks he'd bought for us. The statement said our investment had already grown to about $272,000.

If our account had lost money during a bad stretch we might have paid close attention to it. Sort of like the grocery store that week after week was coming up short of cash. Merchandise gone, unaccounted for. The owners searched and searched and just couldn't figure out how they were losing money. Then one day, somebody looks at the receipts from all twelve cash registers and then counts the registers in the store. There are *thirteen*. The manager had installed the thirteenth register for himself. Terrific thinking, but when you're constantly losing money, the scrutiny is eventually going to catch up with you.

Madoff did the exact opposite. Month after month, you got good news. Two months after we sent him the $250,000, we got a statement that the account was worth $291,000. Why would you want to scrutinize him? The guy never lost. You're thinking: This is almost too good to be true. That's where I should have caught myself. When you're telling yourself it's too good to be true, then it's usually too good to be true.

The biggest reason to have faith in Madoff was that you got your money as soon as you asked for it. I had a large insurance premium to pay a few years back. The same day my accountants requested the money—*bam!*—it was wired to my account. Madoff could do this, of course, because so many other people were giving him money that he wasn't really investing. It's estimated that $170 billion rolled through his offices at one time or another.

Should I have paid attention to the one guy who didn't trust him and made a public squawk? Of course! But everybody else ignored that guy, too. Nobody else asked the basic questions. *He's handling billions of dollars and not dealing with any of the top accounting firms? Why are Madoff's accountants three guys from Queens?* Those are questions you don't ask when winning statements come in month after month.

What you do is spread the good news. It's only natural that you'd want to tell your brother about Madoff. Now, my brother was interested. Only—get this—my brother's money wasn't good enough. Madoff rejected him. Freddie called back and said, "Sorry. What can I say? Bernie doesn't just take everybody."

Are you going to pull out your money in anger? No. It's Madoff's business. It's his prerogative. And it's just your luck to be one of the chosen.

If the economy had continued rolling along, Madoff would have remained undetected. But when the financial meltdown hit in the autumn of '08, requests came in for billions. I try to imagine what that must have been like. This is going to sound crazy, but when I think of myself stealing, the first thing that comes to mind is a Duncan yo-yo.

When I was a kid, all my friends had Duncan yo-yos. You could hear the zing of a Duncan. My yo-yo didn't have any zing to it because it was cheap. So one day I cased the yo-yo aisle at Woolworth's. I waited until just the right moment, then put a beautiful red Duncan in my pocket. The walk to the door was perilous. Perilous! I can still remember the pounding of my heart. If someone had screamed, "Hey, kid!" would I have run for it? I don't know. I was a good kid and well known in the neighborhood. Maybe I'd have tried to squirm out of it. *"Ohhhh jeez, sorry, I was going to pay for it."*

There's just no comparison between my yo-yo and the billions Bernie Madoff stole—which is one reason I'm so curious about him. It's exactly why crime is so fascinating. We all wonder: How could he do that?

Here's what really puzzles me. Madoff knew he was going to get caught the minute he couldn't make a payment. If you're that cunning, why not get on a plane and go to Brazil? There's no extradition from Brazil. Why not call your family and say, "Who wants to go with me?" Or just tell them, "You can visit me in Brazil." It's not a tough choice. You're one of the most hated men in the world. And who hates you? The Jews that you stole from. They're not gonna kill you. It's not like the Italian Mafia. So it comes down to, *Let's see. I'll spend the rest of my life in prison. Or else I'll go to Brazil.* That doesn't seem like much of a choice to me.

I talked with the guy who wrote a *New York* magazine article about Madoff that was headlined BERNIE MADOFF, FREE AT LAST. The story was called that because Madoff had told the Securities Exchange Commission that his last seven years had been a nightmare. He always knew there was going to be a knock on the door, and when it came, he said, it was a relief.

You really wonder what was going on in his mind. He'd

wiped out friends. Destroyed charities. Caused investors to commit suicide. Would it be possible to see him differently if we knew his side of the story?

I've always wondered what the outcome would have been if OJ had been found in the driveway after the murders screaming for the police. What if he'd fallen down on his hands and knees next to the bodies of his wife and the waiter, with the bloody knife in his hand, and the police had arrived to find him sobbing, *"What have I done? I was in a rage and I lost it! I'm guilty! Punish me! I deserve to die!"*

Americans are very forgiving. I believe they'd have forgiven OJ over time. He'd have done a few years for the murders, written a book, and become the number one expert on rage. *What came over me?* He'd have been on every show. The audience would have cried. The audience would have applauded. OJ could never have smiled in public for the rest of his life, but he might have been able to help a lot of people.

It's difficult to imagine how Madoff could ever be seen in a sympathetic light. Especially after he told fellow prisoners that his investors deserved what they got because they were greedy. All con men take advantage of people's greed. But greedy charities? When Freddie Wilpon sees an old boyhood friend at the stadium, he screams at him for buying tickets. *Why didn't you call? I would have gotten you tickets.* Freddie Wilpon is not a greedy man. I've had lunch with Freddie Wilpon many times since the Madoff house of cards came down. There's probably no way to describe the sense of betrayal Freddie feels. Not only for the problems Madoff caused to his finances, but for all the friends who suffered after Freddie brought them in.

Looking at all the damage that Madoff inflicted, I can see how lucky I was. Overall—after putting in, taking out, putting in and taking out—I lost about $780,000. About $280,000 of that was to Madoff. The other half million was money paid in capital gains taxes on stocks I never owned. I gave the government the capital, without ever getting the gains. The government refunded that money. Then the trustee in the case sent a check for the remainder. I feel for the people who never got back what they lost. If I'd been wiped out of everything I had, I'm sure I'd feel what they feel. But at this point, any anger I have has been overcome by sheer curiosity.

I'd like to know what inspired this. How did it start? There are endless questions. I don't know what his answers would be—and I never guess. So I don't know where my questions or follow-ups would take us. No matter how you feel about Bernie Madoff, you can't help but be curious. Because there's probably never been anyone quite like him. There's got to be more to this than we can imagine. I'll tell you why.

One of the most memorable interviews I ever did came about because of a series of stolen bicycles in Central Park. It was with a New York City policeman during the early days of CNN.

I had no idea what to expect. The policeman was in public affairs. He arrived in a wheelchair. He came in with his beautiful wife and a little boy. He was paralyzed from the neck down. His son could touch his face, but he couldn't feel his son's touch. He explained that his father was a cop and his grandfather was a cop.

So, I asked, what happened?

He described how he and his partner were in a squad car riding around Central Park on the lookout for bike thieves when they spotted this black kid with a brand-new Schwinn.

He got out of the car to approach the kid, and the kid shot him. He remembered the smoke coming from his chest. He fell down in a heap. His partner ran over and grabbed the kid. An ambulance arrived. So did a Catholic priest, who gave him his last rites. He was brought to the emergency room. The doctors saved his life. But he was now paralyzed.

Subsequently, the kid got convicted of attempted murder. He was a juvenile who'd never had a record. The sentence was split: some of the time he had to spend behind bars would be as a juvenile and the rest as an adult.

After the cop recovered somewhat, he thought: I want to go see the kid. He went to the jail and he said to the kid, "Why did you shoot me?"

The kid said he was sorry. Then he starts to explain. "I worked in a grocery store part time. I was an A student. I had just bought the bike. My brother—he's the bad guy. He was running out of town and he told me to hold his gun for him. I had never held a gun in my life. He said, 'Hold it for me,' and he left.

"I put the gun in my little pack, and I went off on my new bike. And you were the fifteenth cop to stop me because I had a new bike. I'm glad you came, because I want to ask you something. If I were white, would you have approached me?"

The cop told me: "I had to take a look inside myself and honestly say: 'I would not have approached him if he were a white kid riding on a new Schwinn.'"

The two of them bonded, and the cop became that kid's big brother, and that kid later became a cop. I'll never forget that older cop crying as he told the story.

One of the reasons I like the story is it tells me that something good can come from anything. In the end, life always comes down to how we can help others.

Willie Sutton went on to work for a safe company to design safes that thieves couldn't break into. He also helped wardens design escape-proof prisons. If Madoff conducted classes on how to spot white-collar crime, aren't there people who'd attend? A mind like Madoff's could do a lot of good. Maybe there's a way to monetize it to help pay back those who lost their money.

I'm going to be doing four specials a year for CNN. I've written Madoff quite a few letters requesting an interview. On the surface, there doesn't seem to be any plus for Madoff to sit down with me. Maybe it has no meaning for him. On the other hand, he didn't say, "I'm sorry" in his contrition statement to the judge. I'm not going to put words in his mouth, but if he ever did feel that way, he'd have the chance to say those two words.

I wouldn't be coming to hurt him. I don't like what Madoff did. But I don't know him. I might like him. He's a rogue. I like rogues. I'd certainly treat him fairly. People have always accused me of throwing softball questions. But if I started an interview with: *"Good afternoon, Bernie Madoff, you're a creep,"* what would I learn? I just want to know how it happened.

I'm sure he wants to protect his family. I had lunch with his wife's lawyer. He said that she didn't know a thing. What must her life be like? One minute you're living like a billionaire, the next minute the beauty parlor won't take your appointment, and the restaurants won't give you a table. And every day it keeps getting worse. The day before her son was led to believe a *Wall Street Journal* article would appear with information that he was about to be indicted, he committed suicide in front of his two-year-old son.

It's not easy to have to answer the question, Do you have regrets over your son's suicide? But I don't know how Madoff would respond. Maybe he'd blame the *Wall Street Journal*. There are so many ripples and complexities. I myself wonder if the people who wrote the *Wall Street Journal* story—that, in the end, never implicated the son—felt any guilt when Madoff's son committed suicide. I remember when the investigative reporter Jack Anderson broke a very legit story about a white-collar criminal. The criminal killed himself after the story came out. Jack couldn't rationalize it. It's not like the guy had ever killed anybody. He'd stolen money from some agency. It made Jack very depressed.

There are so many complexities. Maybe there's no upside to talking—except the one that must have occurred to Wesley Snipes now that he's behind bars. When you realize it's helpful to talk, you don't want it to be too late.

There is a lawyer at our table at Nate 'n Al's who brought to breakfast a list of similarities and coincidences in the assassinations of Abraham Lincoln and John F. Kennedy. It's been almost a hundred and fifty years since Lincoln was shot. But you couldn't help but be fascinated.

Lincoln's name has seven letters.
Kennedy's name has seven letters.
Lincoln was elected to Congress in 1846.
Kennedy was elected to Congress in 1946.
Lincoln was elected president in 1860.
Kennedy was elected president in 1960.
Lincoln had a secretary named Kennedy.
Kennedy had a secretary named Lincoln.
Lincoln lost a child while living in the White House.
Kennedy lost a child while living in the White House.
Lincoln was shot in a theater built by Ford.
Kennedy was shot in a car built by Ford.
Lincoln was succeeded by a southerner named Johnson.

Kennedy was succeeded by a southerner named Johnson.
Andrew Johnson's name has thirteen letters.
Lyndon Johnson's name has thirteen letters.
Andrew Johnson was born in 1808.
Lyndon Johnson was born in 1908.
Lincoln was sitting beside his wife when he was shot.
Kennedy was sitting beside his wife when he was shot.
John Wilkes Booth was born in 1839.
Lee Harvey Oswald was born in 1939.
John Wilkes Booth's name has fifteen letters.
Lee Harvey Oswald's name has fifteen letters.
Booth ran from the theater and was captured in a warehouse.
Oswald ran from a warehouse and was captured in a theater.
Booth was killed prior to trial while in police custody.
Oswald was killed prior to trial while in police custody.
Lincoln died on a Friday.
Kennedy died on a Friday.

Two murders, and this is what we're left with. When we don't understand why, we never get tired of wondering. Because when it comes to crime, we're always looking for some thread that will help us understand.

7

Broadcasting

Very often people are disappointed when they get to meet their heroes. Their heroes just can't live up to their expectations. I'm lucky—that's never happened to me. Mine have always treated me in a way that made me proud.

I went to visit one of them at the beginning of my final year on the show. He was ninety-one at the time and in a wheelchair. But whenever I see Mike Wallace, I picture myself as a young man in Brooklyn racing home to watch his show. The show was called *Night Beat*.

Mike's broadcasting approach was very different from mine. *Night Beat* was sort of an attack show. Mike would sit in a chair, smoke a cigarette, and grill his guest. It was a forerunner to what he would do on *60 Minutes*. Mike was intelligent, did thorough research, and had all the facts at his command. The clarity of his delivery made him impossible to click off. He once did an interview with Governor Orval Faubus of Arkansas after Faubus refused to follow federal law and integrate the state's schools, not long before President Eisenhower sent in troops.

The show was nearly always confrontational, and more than a few guests walked off the set in the middle of it. Since they knew the grilling was coming, it was always a mystery why people agreed to go on in the first place.

The comedian Sid Caesar once did a famous takeoff of *Night Beat* on *Your Show of Shows*. Here's the setup: Sid's all ready for his interview with Mike Wallace. But his friends are advising him against it. "Why are you going on? Why would you do this to yourself?"

"Are you kidding?" Sid says. "What's he going to do to me? I've got nothing to hide! No problem!"

So Sid goes on the show. Carl Reiner is playing Mike Wallace. Carl goes through the introductions while Sid waits confidently.

The first question is something like, "Who was Mildred Finnech?"

And you see Sid squirm. "Ohhhhh, jeeez. Oh, God!"

"And your income tax returns from 1952 . . . ?"

"Ohhhhhhhhhh, jeez!"

Soon, water is pouring down Sid's head as if he's sweating profusely. More than fifty years later, the image still makes me smile.

That parody was the ultimate compliment. *Night Beat* was built on the basics of broadcast journalism: Mike came in with facts and questions, and the guest sat across from him with his own viewpoint. The groundwork was laid for a fair exchange. There was a balance.

Time and changes in our culture have chipped away at that balance. If you want to see how much we've lost, all you have to do is turn on Fox News Channel. When I watch Glenn Beck, I see a total circus. I don't buy the act. Fox News lies to suit itself. The most obvious lie is that it promotes itself as "fair and balanced." And MSNBC ain't exactly balanced, either.

When I look back, it's hard to believe all the changes I've seen in broadcasting. I can remember when televisions first came into showrooms. I'd stand in front of the window of a store on 86th Street and stare at the test pattern on the screen. The networks had very few programs, and nothing came on until five o'clock. You waited for that test pattern to flicker. That's how you knew a show was starting. All the television stores piped the sound into the street.

When I think of brilliance in broadcasting I think of Edward R. Murrow. He ended Senator McCarthy's Communist witch hunt with one of the great broadcasts of all time. He didn't argue with McCarthy. He didn't harangue. He let McCarthy bury himself with his own words. *That* was balance.

There were only three networks when I came up in the business. It's always preferable to have more options. If you're a baseball fan, you'd love the ability to tune in to any game being played. We didn't have those benefits, but there were good fundamentals. News was civilized. There were no pundits. There was analysis. A broadcaster had time to build trust. When Walter Cronkite turned against the Vietnam War, the nation turned with him because it respected his judgment.

I don't want to make it sound like broadcast news was perfect back then, or that we should return to those days. When I started in radio, you couldn't even say the word *pregnant* on the air. You had to say *she's with child*. (There was a reason Lenny Bruce came along.) But for the most part, there was respect for the craft, and there were sensible rules. I loved the equal-time amendment. We had to give equal time to opposing points of view during political campaigns. My all-night radio show was very fair. We kept time: if a caller attacked a candidate, that candidate was offered the same amount of time to respond.

Cable changed the whole landscape. Cable is wired underground, so it's not subject to the same Federal rules as companies using the airwaves. There's no equal-time rule for cable. The industry makes its own rules. That not only opened the door to alternatives, but it also opened the door to extremes. Jon Stewart says that Fox is not a network; he believes it's a political party. I agree with him. In a sense, during the final days of *Larry King Live*, I was a broadcaster competing against two political parties—MSNBC on the left and Fox on the right. You always hear on Fox how Sarah Palin and the Tea Party energize the base—Fox's base. CNN doesn't have a base. We're middle of the road. We have a core audience.

I'm not saying the new landscape is wrong. Change is not wrong. In fact, change is the only constant. Music has changed over the years. I used to know every song in the Top 40. Now I don't know any. And I don't think I could ever play along with the tune of today's broadcasting. Bill O'Reilly brings on a guest with little intention of listening to that person's point of view. The guest is merely a prop for O'Reilly to sound off. It's all become theater.

I've never begun a show with an agenda. If one of the suits had ever asked me to yell at a guest, I wouldn't do it. The fundamentals that I brought to my show may be out of vogue, but I'm not going to change. I don't offer a point of view. I try not to use the word *I*. And I ask short questions. My motto is: I've never learned anything while I was talking.

Cable changed the nature of broadcasting in other ways. As the number of channels expanded, so did the competition for viewers. There's always been competition. When I was a kid, movie theaters would actually stop a film in the middle to play the *Amos 'n' Andy* radio show. That's how big *Amos 'n' Andy* was. If the movie theater didn't play *Amos 'n' Andy*, the audience wouldn't show up—everyone would stay home to watch it on television. The theaters adjusted, and people got what they wanted. But going from three networks to a five-hundred-channel universe is not an adjustment. It's a tsunami—and I'm not sure we can recover what's been lost.

There have always been critics of television. I can remember criticisms from the earliest days—especially from the world of print. They'd say that shows were created simply to attract viewers. But, hey, you could say the same about the *New York Times* masthead. Why is there white space around it? To attract you! That white space has nothing to do with the news. The communications business has always been in the business of attraction. But there are now so many people screaming to be looked at it's changed our culture. And as comedy has become mean-spirited to call attention to itself, Glenn Beck and Rush Limbaugh will say just about anything to keep their audiences wondering what's next. More and more, conventional news has succumbed to the tabloid.

I've never tried to force myself into anybody's private life against his or her wishes. Yet I found myself in the center of the collision between tabloid and traditional news the moment O.J. Simpson drove down the interstate in that white Bronco. It was a sensational tabloid celebrity story. But it was also a profound news story. O.J. Simpson was the most famous person ever charged with murder in the history of the world. More than that, it was an everything story: a mystery story, a sports story, a pop culture story, a husband-wife story, a science and technology story when DNA evidence was introduced at the trial, and a father-son story when it focused on the murdered waiter and his dad. Ultimately, it was a story about the way race was perceived in America. I was on the air when footage of the chase came in. People stuck with CNN because they knew our reporting could be trusted.

But many of the lurid stories that broke in the Simpson case were first printed in the tabloids, and television felt compelled to compete. I don't think the media has ever been the same. The line between public and private has become so blurred that sometimes it's difficult to see it at all. The development of the Internet has only intensified the battle for eyeballs. News on twenty-four-hour cable is no longer news. It's "breaking news." The reality is that much of the time it's neither breaking nor news. But the networks have to call it breaking news because if they don't they'll feel left behind the "breaking news" being churned out by the others. The suits live and die by the ratings.

Nobody ever pressured me for ratings at CNN. My producer protected me. Those pressures were on Wendy's shoulders. If I had a choice, I'd do the show the way Charlie Rose does his on PBS. Charlie has the best job in television interviewing. No commercials. He can book any guest he wants. A ballet dancer today, the consul general of Mexico tomorrow. He's not driven by ratings. But that's public broadcasting. *Larry King Live* played on a different field. Cable news is endless and relentless, and the grab for your attention gets fiercer by the day.

Celebrity and political scandals are an easy grab. In just the last year of my show, I had to deal with scandals in the personal lives of Tiger Woods, John Edwards, Sandra Bullock, Lindsay Lohan, Mel Gibson, and the governor of South Carolina, who left his wife for a woman in Argentina.

Many of those shows were newsworthy. Others invaded people's privacy and made me uncomfortable. For me, the line between public and private is generally not blurry at all.

Tiger Woods? No story. There was no crime in Tiger's driveway. Whatever happened between Tiger, his wife, a golf club, and their car is a private matter. Of course, I called up his lawyer to try to get Tiger to come on the show. I certainly understand the importance of having him on as a cultural figure. But is what happened to him relevant to our society? No. This is where that sense of balance becomes lopsided. Four Americans died in Afghanistan yesterday. Would you really call Tiger Woods's troubles with his wife our number-one priority?

The problem is, Tiger opened the door to all that coverage himself. If he had come out right after it happened, he could have put the story behind him. That's what a lot of these advisers don't understand. On the second day afterward, all Tiger had to do was come out and say, "I've had a problem with women. I'm trying to work it out with my wife. Maybe we'll be able to make it work. Maybe we won't."

That's all he needed to say. If he'd done it that way, Tiger would have owned his own story. But it never happens that way. People in that situation crawl into a shell and then they lose ownership of their own life. The media takes it away and profits from each new revelation. Now Tiger's life is in the hands of talk show hosts, public relations experts, and pop psychologists. At that point, the best thing Tiger can do is accept my invitation, or Oprah's, and come on to honestly take his story back. If he does it that way, I'm going to treat him fairly. But unless he decides to open that door, I don't believe we belong in his private life, or in his wife's private life, or in his children's private lives.

Now, *if* you're invited in, everything changes. I had a wide-ranging discussion with Judith Exner about her sexual relationship with President Kennedy. In a case like that, I had no problem asking about details of their encounters for two reasons. One, Kennedy was an elected official. We put him in office. We paid his salary. And two, Exner wanted to clear the air before she passed away. She wanted to leave behind the truth.

Sandra Bullock, on the other hand, didn't want to come on to talk about what it's like to be cheated on by her husband at the height of her career. So what's the point of discussing her difficulties? And just whom am I going to discuss them with? "Experts" who really don't know anything about her personal life, or her husband's? Hanging an entire show on a thread of fact is nothing more than gossip. I've always hated gossip.

If John Edwards is a movie star and fathers a child out of wedlock—I have no interest. But I sure do if it comes up while he's running for president. Then it's important. It's important because people will vote for John Edwards. What if he had been elected? He might have had to resign in disgrace. He could have been impeached over the controversy. The whole country could have been thrown into turmoil. He had to know his actions were going to surface at some point. His wife still wanted him to run even though she knew some of the details. When that happens, the story is about everyone involved.

I'd love to have John Edwards sit down for one of my specials. I still believe he is committed to the issues he stood for in his campaign. I still believe he cared about the poor. For Edwards to get a friend to say he was the father of Edwards's child—how did that happen? How does he look back on everything that transpired now that his wife has died of cancer? These are natural questions we'd all like answered. But if he hadn't been asking for my vote . . . it would have been none of my business.

There are tricky situations. Mel Gibson's not running for

president. Nobody's voting for Mel Gibson. If you are upset by the reports that he beat and threatened his lover, you can stay away from his movies. I'll be honest, I didn't feel comfortable when my producers booked Gibson's lover on my show with portions of what she claims were their recorded phone conversations. She said she recorded the conversations because she thought he was going to kill her and she wanted to leave behind evidence. If you listened to the crazed voice on the tapes, you couldn't be certain that it was Mel's, but it was certainly scary. She said Mel had punched her around and knocked the veneers off her teeth, that one of them went flying into their daughter's face. As much as I felt uncomfortable doing the interview, I couldn't help but be fascinated. I guess that's the problem. But I was always very conscious of the fact that Mel wasn't there to defend himself. Don't misunderstand. I'm not defending Mel. If what his lover said happened, he has to be held accountable. But I always remind myself: Television is not a courtroom. The battle between Mel Gibson and his lover for custody of their child belongs in the legal system—and should be reported from there. Our show probably got good numbers. But that doesn't mean I felt good about it.

One of the last interviews I did about our tabloid culture was with Angelina Jolie. It aired the night after I interviewed Wesley Snipes. One of the questions producers wondered about beforehand was how Angelina felt about breaking up Brad Pitt's marriage to Jennifer Aniston. This was another tricky situation because I didn't want to ask.

Lauren Bacall once told me about the start of her relationship with Humphrey Bogart while she was young and single and he was a married man. He had passed away years before, and she was open to discussing it. This time, I refused to go there. I've spent time with Brad and Angelina in New Orleans and know how they feel about their privacy. Few people on earth are more harassed by paparazzi than Angelina and Brad. The dynamics of their marriage are really none of my business—unless she or Brad wants to talk about it. My instincts were correct. The conversation turned to privacy—and how to protect it.

Angelina mentioned that when celebrities are photographed in France with their children, the children's faces are blurred in publication. I would favor a law like that. Angelina thought legislating distances might be workable. Photographers have long lenses. They don't need to be in the celebrities' faces—and especially not their children's. She knew that the beast would never be stopped. But at least it could be controlled.

Over the years, I've always been very good to the paparazzi. I've generally stopped to talk to people who have approached me in the street with running video cameras. But those incidents were isolated. Until my wife and I filed divorce papers, these people had never hounded me like they do movie stars.

I remember a story that Anthony Quinn told me about the papazzi and Sinatra. Once, Quinn stepped in front of the photographers who were badgering Frank and tried to reason with them. "Here's a man who has brought you infinite joy," he said. "When he is singing a happy song, he makes you feel happier. When you are low, and he sings low, he understands your depth. He hasn't forced you to listen to him. He has a gift and he has chosen to give it to you. You can accept it. Or not. Pay for it. Or not pay for it. Wouldn't you want him to be happy?"

When it became obvious that they didn't care whether he was happy or not—Frank fought back. Once Frank went out cruising on his boat with Mia Farrow. One of the paparazzi got wind of the outing, rented a boat, and snapped away.

After the photos were published, Frank told his associates to find out the name of the photographer. They found out all about him. Then Frank hired eight photographers to follow that guy around the clock and shoot him for two weeks. All night long, they were flashing outside the guy's house. Drove the guy nuts.

That's when you understand it. When it's happening to you.

The night shortly after Shawn and I filed for divorce we both went to see our son Chance play in a Little League game. A horde of paparazzi pinched in on the field. It was a night game, and the mob wouldn't stop flashing. The umpire stopped the game and called the park ranger. We're talking about kids, here. What happens if a flash goes off, distracts a batter, and the poor kid gets hit in the head with a fastball? Still, the paparazzi didn't back off.

I suppose you could say, "Well, Larry, why didn't *you* leave?" But what kind of signal would that send to my kids? They're already going through the trauma of seeing their family separated. Now we can't even be there to support Chance at a Little League game?

There's just no winning. During the chaotic scene when we were trying to get to our cars, and my mother-in-law was knocked down, I couldn't do a thing. I'd been instructed by security to keep my hands in my pockets and not say a word.

From the time I was a kid my friends called me Zeke the Creek the Mouthpiece because it rhymed, and I was an endless flow of words. But I now know what happens in a world of no privacy. *Shhhhhhhhhhhhhhhhhhhhh.*

Which brings me to the tabloid stories around the separation. First of all, I believe what happened between my wife and me is nobody's business but our own. If I didn't feel comfortable asking those questions of my guests, why would I let anyone ask them of me? But I do want you to know a couple of things. A lot of the information that has appeared in the tabloids was not true. Or, in some cases, tiny truths were blown up into giant lies.

Years ago, Elizabeth Taylor came on my show after the tabloids reported that she had Alzheimer's disease and was about to die. She laughed. That's the best way to debunk those stories. I publicly denied a lot of the reports. But it's like Paul Newman told me: They can ask you if you beat your wife. If you say no, then the headline reads, NEWMAN DENIES BEATING WIFE.

Here is the most important thing I can tell you about the experience. A man I had breakfast with every day, who didn't like my wife, who wanted to see me divorced, and who was in need of money, admitted on his deathbed that he had sent information about Shawn to the tabloids. His information was tainted. One of his final wishes was for forgiveness.

We did forgive him. I forgave him because I've always felt it's better to make the best of the situation. I've made a lot of mistakes in my time. But I've always tried to correct them. I have been married eight times to seven women. I have regrets. I have a son who I didn't get to know until he was in his mid-thirties. He is now the president of my cardiac foundation, and I couldn't feel closer to him. I missed his childhood. He sat in a seat at Miami Dolphins games as a boy and looked up at the press box where I was announcing and wondered if he'd ever get to meet me. I had no idea. Just recently, when I was honored by the Dolphins, it gave him great joy to go to the game with me and watch me broadcast from the booth.

The fact is, while late-night comedians were making fun of me, while articles and shows made it look like Shawn and I were through, the two of us took a couple of weeks off to drive up the California coast. We toasted marshmallows. We worked things out.

Nothing else about our marriage should really matter to the public. If this seems like I'm copping out, so be it. I know better. If I tried to publicly clear the air, I'd only rake things up and set off another media frenzy. All that matters to me at this point is that things are right in my own home.

As for the bigger picture? This is what I've taken away from my experiences with the media on a grand scale: I can see three forces moving fast, picking up steam, and about to collide.

The first is the eat-it-up, spit-it-out culture we now live in. *60 Minutes* is one of the most respected and longest-running shows on television. We all benefited from watching Mike Wallace. It's been on for more than forty years. But I don't think the show would even be given a chance if it started now and got the initial reaction that it did back in 1968. It bombed at first. CBS had to stick with it and find the right place for it in its lineup. Now, if a promising new show doesn't get eyeballs, it's gone in a finger snap. A lot of good is going to be lost.

The second concern is about what will happen when the Internet and the television screen come together: When we enter a universe of a million screaming channels—watch out.

And the third is what George Orwell predicted in *1984* and Rod Serling touched on in many episodes of *The Twilight Zone*. A society without privacy may very well create a culture of zombies. *Shhhhhhhhhhhhh.* Someone's listening . . .

I don't know what the world will look like if and when these three forces collide. But I'm glad I'm not going to be around to see it.

8

Politics

A little tip to my replacement. If you're ever going to interview Barbra Streisand—do it live. At least then you'll know
when you're going to start.

I learned my lesson years ago when we set up a taped
interview with Barbra at the Plaza in New York. She tried
on many different dresses, changing over and over for hours,
checking how each one looked not only in the mirror, but
on camera. This is a woman who once taped twelve versions
of "Happy Birthday" for Frank Sinatra. I mean, come on, it's
"Happy Birthday"!

So finally, we're about to start the interview. Ten, nine,
eight . . .

"Hold it!" she screams.

"What's wrong, Barbra?"

"Do you believe those flowers?" she says.

"What?"

"Yellow flowers," she says. "That's just not the right
color . . ."

The only way to keep your sanity is to play along. I smashed my hand down on the desk and screamed, *"Who the hell brought those yellow flowers?"*

She drove me nuts. But then, she made me think about it. As Barbra said, "A man is commanding, a woman is demanding. A man is forceful, a woman is pushy. A man is a perfectionist, a woman is a pain in the ass."

One thing's for sure. Barbra's always worth the wait. What a guest! She's great at everything she does. Her voice is one of the wonders of the world, yet she considers herself more an actress than a singer. And she sees with the eyes of a director.

On the Sunday before the final week of my show, we taped an interview at her home in Malibu. *At least,* I thought, *there won't be any holdups because of the flower coordination in her living room.*

Part of the interview was about a coffee-table book she'd written about designing her New England–style home. It's part barn, part cottage, and part mill house with a water wheel, all set along the Pacific Ocean. Barbra took fifty-seven thousand photos—that's right, fifty-seven thousand!—to document getting it just the way she wanted, right up to the eagle weathervane on the roof. There's a painting of George Washington that our first president actually posed for in the room where we did the interview. Everything was perfect. We were only running an hour and a half late.

It's only natural that someone like Barbra would be passionate about politics—an arena where getting it exactly the way you want rarely, if ever, happens. She's a big D Democrat. So it was not easy for her to watch the trouncing the Obama administration took in the midterm elections. We compared the loss to the one Bill Clinton suffered in his first midterm election. But you never know how events will be perceived later on in history.

I sometimes wonder what I would have thought if I'd witnessed Lincoln's Gettysburg Address. Would I have known it was great? Or would I have been silent like the crowd for a while, then applauded? How would I have viewed it at the time?

When I do speaking engagements, I'm often asked during the question-and-answer session to compare the presidents. It was hard enough in the past to do this because you have to assess not only their situations, but the makeup of the Congress they were working with. Now it's almost impossible. The culture moves too fast.

When I interviewed President Obama during the week of my show's twenty-fifth anniversary, everybody was talking about the oil spill in the Gulf. People were calling it the worst environmental catastrophe in our country's history, and we all wondered when the well would be capped. Now you don't even hear about it. You already don't even hear much about Gabrielle Giffords, the congresswoman in Arizona who was shot shortly after I left my show. These days, everyone's wondering how Obama should deal with Muammar Gaddafi and the unrest in the Middle East. Who knows what will happen from the time I speak these words until the time you read them? In the meantime, our perception of Obama can change daily. No president has ever been scrutinized like Obama is on the Internet. Franklin Delano Roosevelt and Bill Clinton weren't judged by the minute.

This much we know for sure. Obama inherited a country that was in the worst shape it had been in since Roosevelt took office. FDR did major, dramatic things during the Depression. He created projects that put people back to work and revitalized their cities. Firehouses were renovated. Bridges, parkways, and dams were constructed. The post office took on more employees. When people are selling apples on street corners and the song of the times is "Brother, Can You Spare a Dime?" the government is your last hope.

Roosevelt got Social Security passed. Back then, there was no way in America to take care of someone who was sixty-six years old and out of work. Unemployment insurance came from Roosevelt. Right-wingers fought these innovations all the way. "Who's going to pay for this?" they screamed. FDR took a lot of flack. There were a few Republican congressmen who were obstructionists. They tried to block all his plans—and many didn't go through. Roosevelt tried to pack the Supreme Court by adding up to five new justices. The congressmen who stopped him were Martin, Barton, and Fish. So the president went after them in his speeches. *Who would take us down when we try to advance?* Entire crowds would scream: *Martin, Barton, and Fish!* He painted the Republicans as dark enemies of the soul. He didn't seek their friendship. He was less of a compromiser than Obama.

Obama is trying to push through his agenda, but he seems to be doing it from the center—more like Kennedy. That's what has disappointed the liberals. People forget that Kennedy was frustrating to liberals when he first came into office, too. He didn't sign a civil rights bill. He didn't stand with Martin Luther King Jr. during the march on Washington. A lot of liberals didn't want Kennedy to get us into Vietnam. Kennedy sent advisers and sold the war—a decision he would later regret. But you have to remember: Kennedy won the 1960 election by the skin of his teeth. So he was beholden to the center. Obama had much more of a mandate.

He had control of the Senate and the House and a chance to ram through the things that he really wanted. But Obama campaigned much stronger than he governed. His campaign was the very concept of boldness. He made those fiery speeches. *Yes, we can!* But when he got into office he didn't turn *Yes, we can!* into *Now we can!*

Hey, there's no school for presidents. Something happens when the candidate steps into the Oval Office. There's a different point of view. You can relate it to baseball. At first you say, "Let me manage your team. That guy shouldn't play third. I'll put him in center." Then, the first day you put on the uniform, it becomes apparent that you don't have a middle reliever. And you're wondering, How'd I overlook that?

Barbra will tell you: Obama did stave off a Depression. He passed the first major health care bill in seventy-five years. He pulled our troops out of most of the principal cities in Iraq. He bailed out General Motors, settled the economy, and made money for the government in the process. Those were all winners.

He inherited Afghanistan. I don't know how you win there. Prime Minister Putin told me years ago, "I'm not one to give advice—especially to a nation as big as yours. But don't go into Afghanistan. They're indominable fighters. They've got caves to hide in. They love their land and will fight until the end."

Considering the circumstances, you could make a case that Obama had one of the most productive first two years in presidential history. But it didn't look that way to people without jobs or somebody facing foreclosure.

Colin Powell told me that what Obama lacked was a main attack. He said Obama would have been better off if he'd focused on the economy and fixing unemployment to the exclusion of everything else. Not that the other issues weren't important. But it would have put a spotlight on this one area that was vital to every American and given him a clear way to communicate his victories. It could have been a *Now we can!* that opened the door to the other issues, like health care, that were deeply important to him. But because he didn't govern with that focus, his accomplishments were not well understood and he got shellacked in the midterm elections.

It's ironic that the very characteristic that helped get Obama elected—his communication skills—were a disappointment once he got into office. But it makes sense when you look where he positioned himself. It's easy to be a moderate when the economy is good. But people generally don't get roused to action with speeches from the center. They're roused by the extreme.

Think about it. Remember Ronald Reagan in Berlin. "Mr. Gorbachev, tear down this wall!" The resolve in Winston Churchill's voice helped the English stop the Germans in World War II: "Hold forth!" Billy Graham convinced people to swear themselves to God. A lot of us had great expectations for Obama. But we have not yet heard a "There is nothing to fear but fear itself" to rally around.

Lines like that don't come every day.

But Obama's defense of the center looked passive in response to the growth of the Tea Party. It's hard to separate righteous anger from mean-spiritedness. I often don't know where the Tea Party is coming from. But it speaks with an angry voice, and Fox is there to make sure everybody hears it loud and clear.

Can somebody tell me what the Tea Party is all about? They say that God is being taken out of our Constitution. Well, God isn't in the Constitution.

Do they have a leader? A logo? Exactly what are they angry at? They seem to be saying: Bring us back to what never was. What do they want a return to—the days of slavery? I'm not calling anybody I don't know a racist. But there's been so much hatred thrown at Obama, a lot of it hidden beneath the constant questioning of whether he's an American citizen and legally fit to hold office. I'm sure these feelings go much deeper than that. I remember being surprised at the size of the Secret Service contingent surrounding Michelle Obama when she showed up to be interviewed at our studio in Washington.

The comedian Chris Rock said something that I can only hope is true. He said that when he sees the Tea Party it makes him feel like racism is almost over. He compared the Tea Party to the way little kids go crazy just before they go to sleep.

We'll see what happens in the next election. Let's not forget that Bill Clinton is one of the greatest communicators who ever lived—but after his first two years in office, he lost the House of Representatives. Then he came back two years later and romped in the election.

There was a reason they called him the Comeback Kid. It happened over and over in Clinton's career. As governor, he was defeated—not reelected. Then he came back to take the office again. That catapulted him onto the national stage, where he made one of the worst speeches in history—the keynote address at the Democratic Convention in 1988. It was so bad that when he said, "In closing . . . ," he got a standing ovation. Four years later, he won the nomination. And then he came back after the Monica Lewinsky scandal. So you can never count anyone out.

Harry Truman turned it around because of what was seen as guts. When they stopped polling because Thomas Dewey was so far ahead during the campaign in 1948, Truman kept speaking to crowds from the backs of trains. He wasn't a great speaker, but he ran with gusto against the "do-nothing, know-nothing Congress." Later he fired Douglas MacArthur.

A lot of it is sheer determination. A lot of it is simply finding your way.

Obama has two years to find that Clintonesque strategy that recaptured the House in '96. He'll certainly need a Democratic Congress in 2012 to leave his mark. It wouldn't hurt him to be a little gutsier. But I think he's going to be hard to beat in any event because there's no single candidate surging forward on the Republican side. Sarah Palin may win the primaries if she runs against nine guys. But when I interviewed the Bushes, Barbara was very pointed about her. She said, "I think she's very happy in Alaska and I hope she stays there."

I don't think Palin has mass appeal. She scares a lot of people. The Tea Party is still a minority. Fox News reaches only a couple of million people. It doesn't win elections. Neither does Rush Limbaugh. Aside from the Tea Party, the average person doesn't dislike Obama. You may not think he's being effective. But you can't not *like* him. What's not to like?

There will be some budget cutting because of the deficit. The key is to solve the riddle that Mario Cuomo so eloquently presented: You're a family of four. You live in a tenement in New York. Whatever you make each week you spend. You pay the rent, you eat. You have nothing left over. You manage.

There's crime in the neighborhood. Police come by and recommend that you put another lock on the door. The lock costs ninety dollars.

Your daughter comes down with an infection. The cost of the medicine prescribed is ninety dollars.

What do you do?

Do you get the medicine?

Maybe you'll find a way to get the lock next week. You take that risk.

But you're risking your family's security for your daughter's health. That's the other side.

The key is to figure out the way to get both. Maybe that will take a combination of capitalism and socialism. Lyndon Johnson said that this combination is the only system that will ever truly work. I think that's where Obama is aiming, and I hope he accomplishes much of what he wants.

I'm in favor of national health care. I'd like to see wars end. I don't want to see our military in harm's way. We'd have much more money for domestic needs if we weren't policing the world. It would be nice if we were only doing peacekeeping work as part of a UN group. It would be nice to have a strong message from the top that standing up for gay rights puts us on the right side of history. It would be good to see the immigration issue solved. Getting down to 5 percent unemployment again would be a major achievement.

Obama's inauguration was a great moment in history. We'll have that day no matter what happens. It's a symbol of growth. The sad thing is, if he doesn't pull it together during the next two years, he'll be remembered mostly for the opportunity that he had.

9

The Middle East

"I don't want to say Larry King has a lot of experience in the Middle East," a guy once said, needling me at a roast, "but his first interview was with Moses."

Not exactly the kind of compliment you look forward to in life. But the guy had a point. I've seen a lot.

As a kid I dropped pennies into a little blue cardboard box to support Israel. As a young radio broadcaster in Miami I got into arguments when I opened the microphone to the Young Egyptian League. Jews picketed the station. When it came to Israel, they didn't believe an Egyptian point of view had a right to exist.

I got very emotional when I visited Israel. Standing in front of the Wailing Wall, I felt connected to the past. I scribbled my thoughts on a scrap of paper and placed it into a crack between the great stones that had been set in place long, long ago. I don't believe in God, but as a Jew, I had a sense of belonging to something that was far bigger than myself. I felt at home.

On that same trip I also felt a closeness to the Palestinians. All my life I've tried to walk in someone else's shoes. The strange thing is, when I visited the legislator Hanan Ashrawi on the West Bank, the shoes looked very familiar. She welcomed me into her home as if she were my Aunt Dora. *You're not staying for dinner? We cooked all day! There's no question you're staying!*

So many memories . . .

I followed Yitzhak Rabin during his campaign for prime minister—the warrior who turned toward peace. I can remember the night I had to broadcast the news of his assassination. I didn't wear suspenders. I wore a coat and tie.

I argued with the Iranian president Mahmoud Ahmadinejad about the Holocaust.

I've been atop an Israeli tank overlooking the Golan Heights.

I once got a message while I was eating dinner at Mr. Chow in Beverly Hills: "Excuse me, the king of Jordan is on the phone . . ."

The Mossad once nearly killed me by accident. It's turned into a funny story now, but I can just imagine getting to heaven and running into my mother. *Larry, what happened?* "Mom, the Israelis gunned me down." Bottom line is, you don't want to show up on a street in Washington to attend a party for the Israeli prime minister after the Secret Service has assured the Mossad there won't be any traffic.

I've interviewed all the American presidents since Nixon about the Middle East. Jimmy Carter told me how difficult it was to work with Menachem Begin on the Camp David peace accord between Israel and Egypt. Begin dotted every *i* and crossed every *t*. It was always: "Wait a minute! Wait a minute! What exactly does this mean?" Every time Carter got frustrated, he asked himself, *Was my family killed in the Holocaust? I'm supposed to tell him he shouldn't be so methodical? I'm telling him to trust?*

I've gotten to know all the Israeli leaders since David Ben-Gurion. I can still see Golda Meir: "I'm just a simple schoolteacher." Moshe Dayan, the war hero, was the same way: "I'm just a simple farmer."

I interviewed Yasser Arafat when it looked like he might sign the agreement to bring peace. When he wouldn't, the Israeli prime minister at the time, Ehud Barak, looked despondent. Barak told me that the agreement was a great deal for Arafat— but that Arafat probably feared that he'd be assassinated if he signed it.

I looked on once as Muammar Gaddafi entered a hotel suite for an interview. He got the most bizarre introduction I've ever heard: "And now, Brother Leader . . ."

I ran into Israeli prime minister Benjamin Netanyahu soon after I announced that I was leaving *Larry King Live*. "Don't move to Israel," he told me. "You'll get my job."

It turned out that there were other leaders in the Middle East who had to worry about their positions. Less than two months after my show ended, revolutions toppled regimes in Tunisia and Egypt, and unrest spread through the entire region. People ask me where these changes are headed. Everything I've seen in the past puts me in a unique position to tell you: I have absolutely no idea.

For a long time I've felt that no matter what else happens in the Middle East it will always come back to Israel and Palestine.

I once knew a guy, a Jewish theatrical producer born in Israel. When he was a kid, his next-door neighbor and best friend was Palestinian. One of the early wars started, and his neighbor's family feared that the Israeli military would harm them. Messages came from the Arab world. *Leave now, be safe. The might of the Arab world will come and take your land back for you.* So the neighbors decided to pack up and leave of their own accord. The Israeli kid could remember the car pulling away with the Palestinian kid's bicycle tied down in an open trunk. He could remember the expression on the face of his friend looking back.

Then they were enemies.

The violence is wrong. But when I listen to the arguments between the Israelis and the Palestinians it sounds like they're both right.

"Look at the archaeology. This land was ordained to us by God."

"But *we* live here."

There are very few debates where you say, "Good point. . . . Yes, that's another good point." This is one of them. It goes on and on, and it always reminds me of a joke the Supreme Court justice Stephen Breyer passed on. It's about a judge who hears a final argument.

"You're right," he says.

The other lawyer says, "Wait a minute, judge, you didn't hear from me."

"What do you have to say?"

The other lawyer says his piece.

The judge says, "Well, *you're* right."

The first lawyer says, "How can we both be right?"

The judge says, "You're right!"

Bill Clinton told me the Israeli-Palestinian negotiations were the toughest he ever worked on. I have to give credit to George Bush 43. He was the first American president to support a two-state solution. But just as he said it, the Palestinians splintered into two states—turning to Fatah on the West Bank and Hamas in Gaza. And as someone told me, the two sides seem to hate each other more than they do the Jews. So how can the Palestinians find common ground with Israel when they can't find it among themselves?

And it's not as if the Israelis are all on the same page. We used to have a saying: Ten Jews, eleven opinions. Now you've got a fractured government and a deep divide between left and right. Trust will never come easy as long as candles are lit for the millions who perished in the Holocaust. The Jews will always feel like nobody's going to help them—and perhaps they're right. Supposing that Israel were militarily attacked and endangered. With all the shared values, common interests, and relationships between leaders, would the United States send troops to help? Nobody can know for sure.

It sometimes seems to me that Americans have become weary of it all. Ratings for shows about the Middle East have declined over the years. It's as if viewers are saying, "Enough of the killing already!" But after everything I'd witnessed, it seemed appropriate to look at the Middle East through one last show in the final week.

We set it up through the Saban Center at the Brookings Institution. The Center is part of a think tank that generates ideas to help bring about peace. It was created by Haim Saban, an Israeli-American who's one of the brightest people I know. He has a pro-Israel stance—he's one of the country's largest contributors—but I've always believed him to be balanced. He sees the full picture.

That last show on the Middle East could not have discouraged anyone. Tony Blair, England's former prime minister, was the first guest. He'd worked through the agreement between

Northern Ireland and the Republic of Ireland. Many thought they'd never see peace there. "One of the things you learn in this business," Blair said, "is that you can have failure after failure and hit obstacle after obstacle, but you've just got to keep going, because in the end, it can be done." Anyone listening to the Israeli defense minister, Ehud Barak and the Palestinian Authority's prime minister, Salam Fayyad, go back and forth during the hour had to come away with the feeling that if the two were left in a room to work out the problems, they could do it. But they were only two men, and the ground in the region was about to shift.

Nobody who came on the show that day could have known that a few weeks later, a fruit vendor in Tunisia would be slapped in the face by a policewoman and, after his complaints were dismissed, would set himself on fire in protest. Or that this act would set off millions of tweets and Facebook messages. Or that those messages would ignite democratic protests that are ongoing.

When I have any questions about where things are headed in the Middle East, I call Haim Saban. We had a conversation during the recent turbulence. The surprising thing about it was that most of our discussion wasn't about Israel and Palestine. It wasn't about Tunisia and Egypt. It wasn't about Gaddafi's use of foreign mercenaries to gun down his own people in Libya. It was about Iran.

Maybe that shouldn't have been surprising.

After all, Iran's president, Mahmoud Ahmadinejad, had said that Israel should be wiped off the map. Of all the shows I've done over the last few years, the three interviews I did with Ahmadinejad seemed to prompt the biggest reaction in my day-to-day life. I live in an area that's home to a lot of Iranians. As a matter of fact, the mayor of Beverly Hills is Iranian—a good guy. Jews, Iranians, and Iranian Jews have not been shy about approaching me at Nate 'n Al's to vent.

After the first interview with Ahmadinejad, during which I asked about his children, a driver of a car passing me on the street screamed at me for treating the Iranian leader like a human being instead of calling him out as a wannabe Hitler. Before my final interview with Ahmadinejad, in New York, an Iranian woman came over to my table at a restaurant and pleaded with me not to get the American people riled up over Iran. Ahmadinejad, she said, was not the face of her country. The people are good, she said, and they don't deserve to be attacked because of a delusional man who seized power.

Israel's current president, Shimon Peres, told me that he thought Ahmadinejad and Iran had large ambitions in the region. "I don't trust a word he says," Peres said, "but I pay careful attention to what he does."

People have asked me: Do you see Ahmadinejad in the same light as Hitler? That's impossible for me to answer. It may seem like I go back as far as Moses, but I never interviewed Hitler. The closest I ever got was when I interviewed an American newswoman who did during the time that Hitler was a candidate for president. She thought he was passionate, erratic, and nationalistic. Through an interpreter, he warned her to beware of the rise of Communism. He told her that Communism had been fomented by the Jews. But he didn't yell or scream.

I also heard a story about a Jewish photographer who was assigned to photograph Hitler when he first came to power. The photographer saw Hitler in the street and focused the camera just as Hitler turned to look straight at him. The look in Hitler's eyes made the photographer flinch and he was unable to snap the photo. A second later he recovered and he took the picture as Hitler turned away. The photographer never forgot the feeling.

I didn't feel anything like that with Ahmadinejad. I had no fear. He was in America. There was no goose-stepping. He's a short guy with an open collar. It felt like there's some whimsy in him. But looks can fool you.

He's a puzzling figure. I could never get him to respond directly to questions dealing with Israel—or anything else for that matter. Some people stereotype him as a hard-line mullah. He's not a mullah. Ahmadinejad is an academic and he liked to answer my questions with questions. If he's not going to answer the questions, you wonder, why do the interview? But the analyst Fareed Zakaria pointed out that Ahmadinejad was probably not speaking to the American public. He might have done the interviews to speak to the Arab world. His points were well prepared. *The United States has nuclear weapons. Why can you have them and we can't? Why can Israel have them and we can't? Why don't you get rid of yours?* It's hard to argue with that. And you know how that's going to play on the Arab street.

He said that Iran was a peaceful nation that never attacked anybody. Then he pointed out that many of the weapons used against his country when it fought a war against Iraq under Saddam Hussein had come from America. There's no denying that. Ronald Reagan told me that Saddam looked like a good balance against the Iranian regime after it took Americans hostage in 1979.

Ahmadinejad was clever. He sidestepped questions about the brutal measures used to suppress the Green Revolution by comparing it to a recent protest in the United States that had gotten out of hand and was squelched with fire hoses. He'd take a fact that was unrepresentative of a larger truth and use it to make a convenient point. It was like interviewing a cagey lawyer.

What viewers didn't understand is that my show's format was terrible for this sort of interview. We were constantly being interrupted by commercial breaks. So there was no flow. I wanted to get into his mind—not listen to his talking points. But the human aspect becomes very hard to explore when you're being held up by the translations of both question and answer, and then stopped every four minutes for commercials. It's very frustrating.

I felt I was doing a good job when I got him to talk about his children. But some viewers didn't care. They didn't want to see him as a person. Those same people congratulated me after I got into an argument with him in the second interview over the existence of the Holocaust. I didn't feel good about that. Getting into arguments is just not my style. If I'm saying there was a Holocaust, and he's saying there was no Holocaust then nobody is really learning anything. Plus, it's easy to lose yourself in a situation like that. I didn't want to let my buttons get pushed. The host has to stay in control. The only good thing about a moment like that is that it allows the world to see him as he is.

He called Netanyahu a killer of Palestinians. Netanyahu has accused him of killing Israelis by arming Hezbollah to the north of Israel and Hamas to the south. Where might this lead? Would Ahmadinejad use nuclear weapons if he had them? Would he risk an Israeli attack or the world moving in on him?

One reason you can't put Ahmadinejad in a category with Hitler is that he's not in charge. He has a voice, but the mullahs are in charge. And though the Green Revolution was suppressed, you have to wonder how much support the mullahs and Ahmadinejad actually have. So he might have simply been playing to his base when he came on my show. His movement came to power in 1979 after the Shah was overthrown. It came to power with chants of "Death to America!" Maybe coming on *Larry King Live* with an olive branch would have hurt him among his supporters.

It ultimately comes down to statements and actions. When he says there was no Holocaust, you can ignore him. When he says there are no gay people in Iran, you can shake your head and turn away. But if he says that Israel should be eliminated, then it's irresponsible to turn away—and the Israelis have a right to figure out how they're going to protect themselves.

I always want to be optimistic. But sometimes that can be a fault. The problem for the Israelis is that if Iran were to get nuclear weapons there wouldn't be a second-strike option. If Israel was hit with an atomic bomb, it really wouldn't matter if they fired one back at Tehran. Israel is too small. It will go, along with all the Palestinians who now live there.

The Israeli-Palestinian problem may be almost impossible to solve. Yet it may be easier in comparison to the one now being posed by Iran.

I don't want to leave the Middle East on that note. The Saban Center is all about ideas, and I have a few. They're out-of-the-box suggestions that come from everyday experiences and could be applied to any long-standing conflict. They're quite simple. One came to me while I was sitting in a movie theater.

One of the things that everybody knows about the movie business is that people who make movies root against movies made by others. They're always hoping the movie they're up against will tank. But here's the crazy thing. Even though they're hoping that not one seat will fill for their competitor, they make sure to show their own movie's trailer before the other one comes on—just in case there's a packed house.

What if the people of the Middle East could see that working together is to everybody's benefit?

I remember a guy from Sweden telling me he feared the prospect of the Middle East coming together. Its power, he said, would be enormous: all the oil, the Jewish mind for business, the Palestinians' great gift for poetry. What if all the assets in the region could be combined as a single force? If all these people could just join together and help one another, they'd be a world power.

In order to make that happen, millions of people would have to learn how to see others in a completely different way. When I think of this, I think of a snowstorm. A snowstorm and Ted Kennedy.

At the age of thirty-seven, Ted Kennedy had an accident that changed his life. He drove off a bridge around midnight into a pond at Chappaquiddick. The female passenger in the car, Mary Jo Kopechne, drowned. Kennedy said that after he escaped the car, which was overturned on the bottom of the pond, he made several dives to try to rescue Mary Jo, but he didn't report the accident to the police until the next morning. The whole incident was shrouded in mystery. Kennedy received a suspended sentence for leaving the scene of the fatal accident. But the scandal tarnished his image and followed him like a second shadow. I always had the feeling that it was going to be in the first paragraph of his obituary.

Years later, I interviewed a guy who told me a story about Kennedy that only he knew. He was driving on a parkway at night in a snowstorm when he was forced to pull over with a flat tire. A car pulled in behind him. A guy stepped toward him with a jack. It was Ted Kennedy. Ted helped him put on his spare tire. I'll bet that's the first thing that guy thought of when Ted Kennedy passed away.

Ted did something that not many people are able to do. He changed the way a lot of people perceived him. He did it through hard work and earning respect in the Senate. I wonder if there is some way in the Middle East for people to put aside the terrible feelings from the past and focus on a positive future. We're multilayered. We can grow. The Middle East is not so much a region as it is a mass of people. They don't have to see themselves through a cycle of violence. They can believe in change. If not, why sit down and have negotiations in the first place?

Innovative thinking reminds me of the guy who started FedEx. Fred Smith came up with the idea for the company while he was writing a paper at Yale. His professor must have thought he was crazy. *You're telling me that if I want to send a package from Newark to Chicago it's going to fly through Memphis?* Legend has it Smith got a C. But there was a reason he chose Memphis as a hub. It's never fogged in.

Success comes from thinking brazenly. Why don't we have people like Fred Smith and Steve Jobs try to unknot problems like the Middle East? Why don't we take our great thinkers in one area and have them focus on other areas? As the great heart surgeon Michael DeBakey told me: We have guys who design pinpoint bombers. They work with satellites. They figure out ways to bomb one house on a street without touching its neighbor. Don't you think they can pinpoint disease? Don't you think they can make a chemotherapy that knocks out just the right cells without damaging others? What if you used the same intelligence that creates weapons to improve medicine?

Don't you think these people can make an artificial heart? De-Bakey said that if the money we spent on the Vietnam War had gone into the development of an artificial heart, we'd be able to buy one today for about twenty dollars. Amazing things could be done if we had bright fresh minds look at the Middle East in a new way.

And it's not just the CEOs and engineers—it's time to open the possibilities to everybody. I can remember a time just prior to the 1980 Summer Olympics in Moscow. I was doing my all-night Mutual Broadcasting radio show and President Jimmy Carter came on to explain his decision to boycott the games in protest against the Russian invasion of Afghanistan. A cabdriver called in from somewhere like Des Moines. "I'm not one to disagree with a president," he told Carter. "But you could have had it both ways. You could have let the athletes go, only, when they won, they would refuse to step up to the victory stand. *We will compete. We will win. But we will not accept a medal on Soviet soil. We want our medals sent home to America.* That way, the athletes wouldn't be punished. And America would be making a stand every time a winning athlete refused to accept a medal. If you don't go, you don't matter anymore. The event starts and you're history—it's just two weeks of the world watching the Olympics without you being there."

I asked Carter, "Did anyone in the government ever bring up that idea?"

"No," he said, "but it's a very good point."

I'll never forget the look on his face. All those advisers, all those high-level discussions—and it never came up. Leaders can enlist the aid of ordinary citizens simply by listening to them. It's time. Revolutions have been started with Twitter and Facebook.

Maybe we need everyone to sit down as ordinary men and

women and think of what kind of world we'd like to leave behind for our grandchildren. I've been thinking about that a lot lately.

Here's a question that can certainly be passed along in less than 140 characters: Why should any child have to grow up wondering if he or she is going to get bombed?

10

Getting and Giving

Not many people realize that the final show of *Larry King Live* was not really the final show.

We taped a show that aired two days after the finale. It was among a series of favorites that filled out the last two weeks of the year and was called "The War on Cancer."

The principal guest was a man who'd been told he had only twelve months to live . . . eighteen years ago—Mike Milken. The former junk-bond king is now known as the man who changed medicine. As the show unfolded, we ran clips showed Lance Armstrong, Colin Powell, Sheryl Crow, Olivia Newton-John, Joe Torre, General Norman Schwarzkopf, and others discussing the disease. Nobody knew it, but there easily could have been a clip of me among that group. You would have heard me describe what it was like to be laughing over breakfast with my buddies when a call came from my urologist, asking to see me face-to-face. That's how I found out that I had prostate cancer. It was the start of 2010—yet another layer to the wildest year of my life.

Prostate cancer. Men react to those two words in different

ways. Prostate cancer can be a very slow-growing disease. It doesn't have to kill anyone. If it spreads, that's when there's real trouble. Robert De Niro's father made the choice to watch and wait—and died when it quickly spread. De Niro was mad at him. When De Niro himself was diagnosed, he had surgery immediately. So did Joe Torre. Torre didn't want any kind of cancer growing in his body—get it outta there!

My case was puzzling. Dr. Skip Holden maximized it and minimized it at the same time. It's in an embryonic state, Skip said. You're going to live a long time. If you treat this aggressively with radiation, who knows, you could live to ninety-five.

It's always good to get a second opinion. The other doctor I went to see is also top of the line. Dr. Alan Shapiro has an office not far from Skip's. He's got an Ivy League diploma just like Skip. He looked at the same test results as Skip. But he had a very different opinion. He told me the cancer was slow-growing and there was no reason to act on it. "For a man who is seventy-six," he said at the time, "this is not a big thing for you to worry about. Especially when you consider the aftermath of radiation. You're not going to like that."

The radiation treatment is accompanied by hormone shots. You know the old joke about the guy getting hormone shots: Not long after you take one, you want to go shopping. Basically, the treatment kills your cancer cells and your testosterone. Once the radiation starts, Shapiro said, there's a good chance you'll lose interest in sex for a while and maybe forever.

Which way do you go?

Or, as one survivor of prostate cancer bluntly put it: "Would you rather have sex or die?"

If you're fifty years old then it's not a question. If I were fifty I would wipe it out immediately. But at seventy-six? That's when it's tough. I asked a lot of questions. But ultimately, it came down to this: I'd like to give myself the best chance of seeing my two young boys graduate from college.

So I followed Skip's plan of action. I did the radiation five days a week over two months. It's really easy: You lie down. They measure. They play a couple of Sinatra songs while a machine moves around your body and shoots. There's no pain at all. Each session takes about seven minutes.

I was told I'd feel tired. I didn't. I had some trouble with bowel movements. You're constipated for a while. You urinate a great deal. The strangest thing is when a girl in a miniskirt and high heels passes you on the street, and you don't feel anything. It really is like that joke about how your get-up-and-go got up and went.

Something should be said for the wives of the men who have prostate cancer radiation treatment. They have to put up with a lot. I came through healthy. There was a quality of life missing for some time. But things are looking up with treatment. I'll tell you what, though. Every time I read about someone dying of prostate cancer, I feel smart.

There were some amusing moments along the way. A guy told our breakfast gang about the robotic device that had been implanted in his penis after his prostate had been removed. Push a button, and an erection goes up. Push again, and it goes down. His doctor joked that when he dies they'll have trouble closing his coffin.

It felt good to learn that down the road a man with test results similar to mine will no longer face a tough decision on treatment. A cutting-edge study has identified twenty-four types of prostate cancer. Some don't spread quickly and can be left alone. Others are dangerous and have to be attacked immediately. Once a diagnosis process is perfected, each case can be dealt with accordingly.

One of the things Mike Milken wanted to do on the show was thank me for everything I'd done to help make medical advances like that possible. I have a hard time with compliments to begin with, but this really seemed like a stretch. What had I done?

Mike's answer caught me off guard. He brought up the shows we'd done in the midnineties highlighting the March on Cancer in Washington. After one of those shows, three thousand people called in to help. OK, that I might have expected. When General Schwarzkopf goes on the air and tells America that Saddam Hussein killed thousands of people in Kuwait but that prostate cancer kills more, there's going to be a response. But I'm not the type of guy to look at the picture in dollar terms. Mike is.

Mike looked at the cancer research sponsored by the National Institutes of Health. At the time of our first show, the annual budget was $14–$15 billion. Mike said the awareness that followed my shows helped increase that NIH budget to $29–$30 billion.

Think about the additional $15 billion a year, Mike said. Over ten years, between 2000 and 2010, that adds up to $150 billion. It also had a bandwagon effect because others put up money for cancer research as well. This increase in funding shaped the agenda for the battle against cancer in the United States.

It used to be that 95 percent of men with testicular cancer couldn't be cured. Now the cures for testicular cancer are highly successful. The death rate in prostate cancer has dropped from 43,000 a year in the United States before the first March on Cancer to 29,000 a year today. At this moment, twelve million people who once had cancer are living normal lives, in part because that research funding has led to medical advances.

There's still a long way to go. Fifteen hundred Americans die each day of cancer. That's the equivalent of four jumbo jets crashing every day of the year. Last year more money was spent on potato chips than was invested in the National Cancer Institute. Mike was using this last show to keep pressing forward. The way he sees it, the elimination of cancer as a cause of death is worth $50 trillion to the U.S. economy. Most importantly, his own experience has taught him that the greatest gift he can give someone is a life.

I went home that night and talked to Shawn about it. It all seemed abstract to me. The way I looked at it, if there is ever a cure for prostate cancer it should be named after Mike Milken. Mike and his work for faster cures, together with the researchers, doctors, and other medical professionals, are making the difference.

What did I do? Put on my suspenders and ask a few questions.

Over and over, people thank me for these things. It always amazes me. I'll tell you why and give you a classic example. Ryan Seacrest is a good friend of mine. Whenever he gets a chance, he talks about how generous I am. Sometimes he backs it up by telling the story about the day we met.

Now, I'm a pretty good storyteller. In fact, a guy in radio who'd heard Will Rogers once told me that I was the best storyteller he'd ever heard. I definitely can't take that compliment. The story you're about to read is better when Ryan tells it, so here's Ryan's version. After you've read it, you tell me how generous I am.

Ryan Seacrest

I was in the airport in Paris on my way back to Los Angeles when I saw Larry at the security gate. He was going through the metal detector. *Thank you, God,* I was thinking, *this is my one shot!*

I'd been a fan of his show for so many years. I'd wanted to meet him for so long. All I had to do was walk a short distance to ask if I could hang out with him and learn.

So I went over to him. He looked at me as if I were an agent for Homeland Security—like I was about to check his pockets and interrogate him.

"No, no, no," Shawn said. "This is Ryan Seacrest. He hosts *American Idol.*"

"What do you do, kid?"

"Doesn't matter what I do," I said. "I just wanted to say that you're an idol of mine. I really admire you."

He looked me up and down. He was holding a big Louis Vuitton bag full of hardcover books. And he said, "I'm your idol?"

"Yeah."

"Why don't you carry my bag?"

So I grabbed his bag and the three of us started walking through the terminal as if I was the other wing to Shawn. It was Shawn and her two husbands walking through the terminal at Charles de Gaulle.

We finally got to the lounge. Larry sat down.

Shawn said, "You comfortable?"

"I'm good," Larry said.

"Good," Shawn said. "I'm gonna go shopping."

And Larry had this look like, *Don't leave me with this guy. I talk for a living. Now I have to make small talk with this guy at the lounge of Charles de Gaulle Airport?*

She took off.

"So tell me about this show," he said. This was in the early days. "What do you do?"

"It's a TV show. We look for singing stars."

"How often is it on?"

"Two nights a week."

"I do *my* show *every* night."

"I know, Larry, I love your show. I watch it every night."

"I do it *live*."

"I know, Larry. I started in radio."

"You're a radio guy?"

"Yeah."

"*My* show is a radio show on TV."

So we started talking about radio. He and I were starting to bond.

Shawn came back with sunglasses and purses. It was time to go. Once again, I grabbed the Louis Vuitton bag filled with hardcover books, and we headed toward the gate to board the plane. It was really hot. The plane was late, and Larry is not the most patient individual—he'll admit to that.

Turned out we needed to get on a bus to get to the plane. This was new to Larry. He thought we should be boarding straight from the gate.

"Shawn, why are we on a bus? Kid, why are we on a bus? We're supposed to be on a plane. Ask the driver! Where are we going?"

"Larry, we take a bus to the plane. It's no problem—"

"No, no, no. How long?"

"You want me to ask the driver?"

"Yeah. Yeah. Ask the driver how long."

"Sir," I asked the driver, "how long?"

"Ten minutes," the driver says.

"TEN MINUTES!" Larry can't believe it. "We're supposed to be taking off!"

Finally, we got to the plane. The flight was delayed. I was trying to calm Larry down. Shawn was oblivious to all this. She's used to it and she's very patient. So the delay allowed Larry and me to bond a little more.

He said, "You know what? You ought to be a guest on the show."

"I'd be honored. You want me to come in carrying the bag?"

"No, I'm serious. Be a guest."

The flight was preparing for takeoff. I had to go back to my seat. I sat down, and next to me was a guy with body odor so bad that it literally pushed my hair back, which is some strong feat. So after the plane took off I went back to Larry and Shawn and said, "Sorry, I don't mean to bother you. I'm not a stalker. But there's a guy next to me with body odor, and I can't deal with it."

So Larry and I got a chance to bond a little more. We both like jeans. He wears jeans under the desk on his show. He liked my jeans. "I'll send you some," I said.

"Kid, zipper, not button. Because when you're my age, you gotta get out fast."

We bonded some more.

Larry said, "You know, there's one night in the next couple of weeks when I'm not gonna be in town. Why don't you host the show?"

This was going really well for me. I had gone from the bag carrier to a guest host, and we were midway through *one* flight.

"We'll book somebody in the news," he said. "Somebody who will make it comfortable for you, because you know, it's *live*—"

"Yeah, yeah, I got it."

"It's a full hour."

"I've got that part. I've watched."

"You watch my show? Oh, yeah, I'm your idol, that's right . . ."

Of course, Ryan was embellishing a bit there. But let's stop for a moment and take another look at that story. I'm at the airport. I meet a guy. I ask him to carry my bag. Then I ask him to work for me on a night I want to take off. He sends me jeans. For years now, he's been sending me jeans.

And *I'm* a kind and generous guy?

Truth be told, it's not all that much different from what happened with my cardiac foundation. I get a lot of plaudits for it. But let me tell you how it got started.

I went through heart surgery. I recovered. I was sitting down for lunch one day with friends at Duke Zeibert's restaurant in Washington. This was 1988. Someone asked how much my heart surgery had cost. I had no idea. I didn't know because the insurance company took care of all the bills. But it got me thinking. The thing about a bypass is that it's elective surgery. You may have a severe blockage, but your insurance company isn't necessarily going to pay for you to get it fixed. What happens if you can't afford it?

Soon afterward I got a few people together, and we held a fund-raiser at a high school in Baltimore. That's how the foundation got going. Then I met Shawn. She got involved. My son Larry Jr. became president. He has a great business background and he figured out ways to advance the process. Almost every day, the foundation gives somebody the heart surgery that he or she needs but can't afford. And what's my responsibility in all this? I get up with a microphone at fund-raisers and ask people to help. I phone recipients to tell them that they've been selected. Let me tell you something—that ain't generosity. That's pure joy.

I just don't see myself as on the same level as Bill Gates, Eunice Kennedy Shriver, or Bono. Those people have shown fierce commitment. Think about this: Bill Gates and Ted Turner are nearing their goal of eradicating polio. They're working to vaccinate everyone in the world who couldn't get the vaccine before. And Warren Buffett has pledged billions so that the Gates Foundation can do even more.

When I see Bono, I don't see a musician. I see a man who's changing the world. Talk about an amazing journey. He couldn't even read music. He started a band. Then the guy who designs their album covers came up with the name U2. Bono thought a U2 was a submarine. They went with it. When Bono found out it was a spy plane shot down over the Soviet Union, he no longer liked the name. But the band caught on. He started doing Live Aid in the mideighties and ended up working at an orphanage in Ethiopia during a famine.

One night in Ethiopia he woke up in his tent to the sight of tens of thousands of people who'd been walking all night to get food. Sometimes their children arrived dead. I remember him telling me about a guy who'd brought a beautiful boy over to him and asked him to take the child. The guy said something like, "I know my child will live in your hands, but not in mine."

Bono was astonished to find out that some African countries were paying more to the Western world to service their debt than the total of the aid that he was helping to bring in. He then started devoting his life to issues like debt relief for African countries and stopping the spread of AIDS. He speaks with presidents, prime ministers, and the pope as an equal in this process. Now, there's a guy who merits a thank-you.

As does Eunice Shriver. She started the Special Olympics more than forty years ago. She did so out of sheer rage—rage at the way people with disabilities were being bullied. Eunice, Bono, Bill Gates—these are people who have committed their lives to making a difference. Me, I'm a guy who likes to remember the great riffs Lenny Bruce used to do about telethons.

Telethons drove Lenny nuts. He'd pretend to be the agent searching for talent: "Get us the broad that cries! You know, the one that wept during the telethon for educational TV." He did a whole bit on guys looking to start an organization just to make money from the telethons. "We gotta find a disease where there's no chance of a cure. That way we can keep it rolling. You pay doctors to say we're making advances. We set up a lab. The public loves test tubes! And if we have trouble getting talent for the fund-raiser, we'll book radio guys who love to be on television."

I do have to admit that for me, one of the year's most gratifying moments was our telethon after the earthquake in Haiti. It raised $9 million to help the victims. What made me most proud was my staff. We had never done a telethon before—and they put one together in about two days.

You couldn't ask for anybody better to organize it than Wendy. Here's all you need to know about Wendy and organization. Once, she got a phone call in the middle of the night saying she was being evacuated from her home because of fires in the San Diego area. She and her kids rushed out of bed. The kids started looking for the things that meant the most to them to take away. You know what Wendy was doing? Wendy was making the beds. She was making sure all the dishes were just right in the dishwasher. Only Wendy would make a house perfect for a fire. This is a woman who recommends that people create a color-coded schedule on their computers. Appointments for the kids are red. Work meetings come in blue. Personal engagements are green . . .

I can make fun of this all day, but it sure comes in handy when you've got to put together a telethon. Lenny Bruce had no idea how complicated it is. You've got to line up the charities you're going to work with. You've got to build sets. You've got to set up phone banks. You've got to book celebrities to man the phones. That means bringing in hair and makeup people for the celebrities. Every guest brings an entourage with a set of requests. Can't forget the catering for all the entourages. The details are staggering. You've got to book the reporters on the ground. Get the graphics ready. Figure out what music to use. Lock in extra time from the network. Lay out when the commercials are going to air. Forty people on the staff made it happen. All I have to do is say, "And now, let's go to Port-au-Prince and Sanjay Gupta . . ."

But who do you think gets the credit?

When I saw the devastation in Haiti after the quake and I realized the help our audience was sending, I felt good. The sensation reminds me of a quotation from Abraham Lincoln that goes something like this: "When I do good, I feel good. When I do bad, I feel bad. That's my religion."

I don't believe in God. I wish I had faith like Shawn and her father. Believers are in a no-lose situation. They're either going to be in another, better place, and then they'll know they were right. Or they won't be in a better place, and they'll never know it.

The writer Herman Wouk, an orthodox Jew, once told me: "Even if you don't believe, let me show you the genius of God."

"OK," I said, "What's the genius?"

He said, "Saturday is my day of rest. I know that one day of the week, for twenty-four hours, I will have no tension, no pressure, no work. I won't write a thing. I won't hear, "Herman, we need this," from the publisher. I take a breath. I do it for my faith. But you could do it just for a good way to live." That's hard to argue with. Plus, Herman obviously knows something; He's ninety-five.

For me, stepping up to a mike and helping someone in need is simply a good way to live. So I'm always happy to em- cee the fund-raiser for the Las Vegas Cancer Institute. It gives me pleasure to know I've been part of a place where people under intense stress can get treated under blue ceilings that look like a peaceful sky. If I can help Larry Ruvo and the Center for Brain Health in Las Vegas that he dedicated to his father—of course I'll be there. And I'll be there for Bob Shapiro and the foundation named for his son Brent, who could have been saved from a drug overdose if someone at a party had called 911. Bob never stops thinking of his son, no matter what he's doing. "I'm sitting here talking to you. I'm laughing," he once told me. "But Brent is always on my mind." He wants to make sure no parent ever has to feel that way. How could you not help?

I've met the Dalai Lama a few times. When I interviewed him last year, he told me about his recent gallbladder operation. He made sure that everyone understood that he had no magi- cal powers. He couldn't wave the pain away. He saw himself as a simple man. But there was a clarity in his eyes. I believe that clarity came from basic compassion.

When I stop to think about all this, I think of the person to whom I'd like to dedicate this book. You've probably never heard of him. His name is Hunter Waters. He was a producer on my show. He started out as an intern and for ten years worked out of Washington bringing in political guests. The thing about Hunter is he always made me smile. Even when he called to tell me we had lost a guest, I was happy to hear his voice.

Hunter got esophageal cancer. The thing about esophageal cancer is that you don't usually notice the symptoms until stage 4—when it's too late. Hunter passed away at the age of thirty-two, a couple of months after the final show. It's hard for me even to think about it. When I do, I wonder why that $150 billion dollars of research over ten years couldn't help Hunter.

So you see, whatever good I've done in helping to stop cancer, it wasn't enough. We can always do more.

11

The Replacement

When Bill Clinton was in office we taped a show in which we toured the White House around Christmas. Our timing was great because a holiday party was scheduled for later in the day.

I returned for the festivities with Shawn, the broadcaster Tim Russert, and the sportscaster Jim Gray and his wife, Frann.

The guards out in front of the White House checked Shawn in. They checked in Tim. They checked in Jim and Frann. Then I stepped up.

"Sorry, you're not on the list."

"What?"

"We can't let you in."

"But I was here all day."

"Sorry, but we can't let you in if you're not on the list."

"How do I get on the list?"

Obviously, they knew who I was. Obviously, this would all be worked out. So the rest of my group went ahead without me.

Meanwhile, the guards started putting me through the same security procedures you go through at the airport.

It was crazy. As I was going through this, I looked up. There were Shawn, Tim, Jim and Frann, and Sam Donaldson looking down at me from a window inside the White House. They were all waving, with big smiles. You could almost hear them saying, "Hey, we'll be happy to call you a cab . . ."

Suffice it to say, I know what it's like to be on the outside looking in.

One of my final guests was Conan O'Brien. He got a true dose of what it's like to be on the outside looking in when he was pushed off *The Tonight Show*. I've been on Conan's show many times, and we have great chemistry. He asked me to help him with his opening sketch when he started his new show on TBS. It was a hysterical satire of his departure from NBC.

The sketch starts out with Conan on the phone, telling the suits: "You want me to move *The Tonight Show* to 12:05? Forget it! I'm not doing it! Go to hell!"

He hangs up, puts his hands behind his head and says, real smug, "What can they do to me?"

The next thing you know, he's driving his little car out of the office parking lot. He stops at the guard booth. In the background, you can hear music reminiscent of *The Godfather*. The cop inside the booth takes his parking credentials and then ducks out of sight. Remember Sonny at the toll both? Four guys with machine guns pop up from behind the bushes.

They turn Conan into Swiss cheese for like, thirty seconds.

Cut to Conan in the hospital. He's inside a full body cast. A doctor leans over him and says: "The good news is you'll live. The bad news is you'll never work in network television again!"

In the next scene, he's recovered but depressed, at home

with his wife and fourteen kids running around. His wife is going crazy, screaming at him. "Get a job!"

"I don't know how," he says.

He applies for a position in advertising with Don Draper from the show *Mad Men*. Draper looks at his application and says, "You have no advertising experience, and it's 1965—and you're two years old. Get out of my office."

He finds work at a fast food place. He's behind a counter telling a lady customer how great the musical acts on his show used to be. The lady says, "I don't care who you were! I just asked for some extra sweet-and-sour sauce!" He hands her seven forks, and she explodes.

Next, he's reduced to working as a clown at a kid's birthday party. But he bombs when he gives the children a monologue with an Obama joke.

So he's destitute. He goes to the Fourth Street Bridge in Los Angeles and gets up on the guardrail. He's looking down at the river. The boats passing beneath him seem tiny. The wind is blowing. He's just about to take the fatal plunge.

That's when I appear before him wearing angel wings. "Don't do it, Conan!"

(It wasn't in the shot when it played on his show, but a black guy driving by on the bridge slammed his brakes when he saw us. *Holy moly!*)

Conan looks at me.

"*Larry King?*"

"I'm your guardian angel."

"But you're not dead."

"Never mind that. I have two words for you: *basic cable*."

"Basic cable." It dawns on him.

Next thing you know he's negotiating a deal with TBS. His contract says: *Less. Much less.* But he comes out of the office like he's whistling Dixie, everything is going to be OK. Then the same four network henchmen with the machine guns jump out and turn him into Swiss cheese again.

His last words are: "Awwwww, come on . . ."

The timing of his appearance on my show was just right. My final hour was soon approaching, and it was good to talk with someone who could tell me what it was like to be on top of the world one minute and off the air the next.

I admire Conan. He made a deal to take over *The Tonight Show* from Jay Leno years ago. He waited for his time. He had a phone conversation with Johnny Carson before he took the reins. He understood the show's place in history. Then after seven months, the network said, Sorry, we don't like your numbers. Go to midnight. We're bringing Jay back.

Screw you, Conan said. He wasn't going to do anything outside their initial agreement.

There was a lot of debate over the debacle at our table at Nate 'n Al's. Some of the guys felt Jay shouldn't have taken the show back, out of respect for Conan. Others felt that Jay did nothing wrong. He'd made a decision to go on at ten o'clock when Conan took over. That time slot wasn't working for him, either. What was he supposed to do when the network made him an offer to return to *The Tonight Show*? Say no? The network might have replaced Conan with someone else. Where would that have left him?

Both guys used humor to vent their feelings. There were some great lines. I liked this one from Conan: "Hosting *The Tonight Show* has been the fulfillment of a lifelong dream for me. And I just want to say to the kids out there watching, you can do anything you want in life. Unless Jay Leno wants to do it, too."

Jay said, "Conan O'Brien understandably is very upset.

He had a statement in the paper yesterday. Conan said NBC had only given him seven months to make his show work. When I heard that, I thought, seven months, how'd he get that deal? We only got four!"

When he came on my show, Conan admitted to having some bad feelings about what happened. He told me that after he left the show he would occasionally find his mind drifting when he was driving on the freeway and joked that he sometimes took his anger out on the drivers around him.

Jay was still feeling a little awkward about it all when I guested on his show shortly after mine ended. He came through the door of the green room with a big smile and said: "You're the only talk show host I don't get blamed for getting taken off the air."

I invited Jay to come on *Larry King Live* during the last few weeks. But he said he didn't want to seem like he was whining. He's got a good heart. When he found out that I'd been hurt by some of his jokes about me, he phoned to apologize. And when we talked in private about his return to *The Tonight Show*, he said he realized that his overall silence was probably the wrong way to have played it. He should have had some public relations strategy to get out his side of the story.

There are always going to be ill feelings in a competitive business. I remember a story George Schlatter told about a long-running feud between Milton Berle and Bob Hope. The two didn't speak to each other for years and were very old men when they finally bumped into each other.

Hope said, "You stole my Herbert Hoover routine!"

Berle said, "It was *my* Herbert Hoover routine!"

The argument got more and more heated until finally George Schlatter stepped in the middle and asked, "What was the joke?"

Neither one of them could remember. But they stayed furious.

I've never been one to get into those kinds of squabbles. The last fistfight I had was with my friend Herbie over the Dodgers and the Yankees when I was a teenager. I've never gotten into spats on the air. The closest I came was when I was invited on Howard Stern's radio show, and he asked me what it was like to make it with Angie Dickinson.

I wasn't going to go there. So I said, "Just so I get it straight. Is the question from a standpoint of desire or jealousy?"

We started to go back and forth. Howard Stern is a broadcast phenomenon. He's clever. He's funny. But his sense of humor comes from the ribald. He's not Lenny Bruce. I come from the Mel Brooks school. You never want to mess with Mel Brooks. I'm not saying I'm anywhere close to Mel. But I've got a little of what Mel has.

Howard didn't fare too well in the exchange. Finally, his father called in and told him he should know when to quit.

I didn't have any bad feelings about my replacement. Conan felt screwed about being replaced. I didn't. Nothing is forever, and I had decided it was time to leave. So I looked at my replacement much differently. Besides, I had never felt like I cut out the woman *I'd* replaced twenty-five years before. So why would I feel like my replacement was cutting *me* out?

When CNN announced that Piers Morgan would be taking over the nine o'clock time slot, I didn't know what to say. That's because I didn't know much about him. I'd seen him as a judge on *America's Got Talent*. He seemed perfectly fine in that role. But I couldn't tell much about him from that. I'd never seen him interview anyone. So how could I comment?

I'd met Piers once. He was very cordial to me—even reverential. And how can you argue with a guy who gets the job and says, "This is like trying to follow Sinatra in Vegas"? All I could do was wish him the best.

The one thing I didn't understand was why anybody would want to follow someone who'd been at a job for twenty-five years and had a loyal following? It's hard to follow Bear Bryant. I mean, wouldn't it be better to follow the guy who followed the guy? Wouldn't it be better to be Thomas Jefferson than John Adams?

The reaction at Nate 'n Al's—and everywhere else I went—seemed to be puzzlement. Sort of like, How could a guy from Britain become president?

This put me in some ticklish situations. The British angle was fresh meat for a comic like Jon Stewart. "By the way," he said on my show, "they've made a brilliant choice—a British guy nobody's heard of. When I'm thinking about floating a sinking ship, what do I want to bring on it? A guy that people are going to tune in to and say, 'Who's that? And why is he speaking so funny?'" Then, when Anderson Cooper appeared via satellite, Stewart tagged it with: "What country do you think the guy's coming from to replace *him*? Do you think they're going to grab a Romanian?" Jon is very witty and caustic. I didn't share his view. But it *was* funny.

What I had a hard time understanding was the way Piers promoted his show. He was going to be dangerous. I didn't know if that was a bit of British humor, or what. I'd heard he'd interviewed the British prime minister something like fifty-six times. That doesn't happen if you're dangerous.

I wondered how you could possibly be dangerous and get guests. The O'Reillys and the Hannitys don't need big guests.

Their shows are about them. Over the years, so many of my guests told me they'd opened up because they felt comfortable. You learn a lot when people feel safe. Paul Newman once told me that I had it all figured out, that I could relax because it was all about the guest. Paul said, "You know you're going to be here tomorrow."

Maybe CNN was simply trying to separate Piers from me. Maybe it wanted to get across a message that something new was coming. I'll tell you one thing. In Brooklyn, if you say you're going to be dangerous, you'd better be dangerous.

Just as I suspected, I found no danger in Piers's early shows. He asked good questions. I thought he did fine. But dangerous? No.

BBC Radio interviewed me by phone around the time of the London premiere of *Anna Nicole Smith: The Opera*. As the interview wound down, I was asked what I thought of Piers. I said I thought he'd been oversold—which, of course, immediately spread like wildfire all over the Internet.

Naturally, Piers asked me to come on the show when he was out in Los Angeles—and I was happy to do so. There was a slight problem. I was scheduled to coach my sons' Little League team the day that he wanted me on. So I could only do half an hour before leaving for practice.

We sat down. We laughed. Piers gave me a pair of Union Jack suspenders. They were clip-ons, but I appreciated the gesture. I told him I was opening up an Original Brooklyn Water Bagel Co. franchise in Beverly Hills and invited him to join me for breakfast. The invitation wasn't for show—I wish him well, and he's welcome anytime. I'll even teach him to say *water* the Brooklyn way—*wawduh*.

Piers didn't know it, but he gave me another, more important gift that night. He gave me a piece of information that

I wouldn't have known until after my final show. When I arrived to coach my kids it was not yet seven o'clock. Piers was still on. What I realized was that there was no other place on earth I wanted to be at that moment more than on that Little League field.

12

The Finale

The columnist Art Buchwald once introduced me at an awards ceremony like this: "The great thing about Larry King is that he doesn't know he's Larry King." I always thought a good title for my autobiography would be *What Am I Doing Here?* because I can't believe it all happened to me. The final night of my show was no exception.

Larry King Live was going down as the longest-running show with the same host at the same time on the same network in the history of television. But there was no time to sit around and get nostalgic about it. Family and friends had come in from all over the country for the party after the show. Plus, I was dealing with ten- and eleven-year-old boys. You're always a parent first. So I had to weigh in on whether Chance should wear his beret with the brim in front like a ballplayer or behind like an art critic at a French museum. And if I *had* taken a nostalgic moment and lapsed into a song from my youth, I certainly would have heard about it from Cannon. "Dad, why are you singing those oldies from the eighties?" I'm also married to a woman who is on time about as often as I'm late. If the boys and I had waited for Shawn to put on her makeup at home, the world might still be waiting for the final show. *C'mon, you can put your makeup on in the car!* One of the world's great mysteries is how our driver, Daniel, always manages to get us where we're going on time.

The ride over was surreal. Think about it: just to be a seventy-seven-year-old man whose kids are wondering what place they'll have in the batting lineup for their Little League team. Then I looked up and I was passing the street that bears my name as we rolled into CNN's parking lot. There must have been fifty cameramen outside the studio. I stopped for a few minutes to speak with reporters, but I really didn't have any answers. Of course, I wasn't exactly feeling great. I'd been doing the show for twenty-five years—almost a third of my life. There was nothing happy about leaving. For me, there's never been any joy in the word *goodbye*.

As I entered the building, staffers broke into applause. That was hard. Even though I knew I'd be coming back to do specials, there was no escaping the fact that this was the last time I'd be seeing many of them. But my head was constantly turning to see what my kids were up to. *Cannon's in Greg's office. Where's Chance?* Ninety-year-old parents have told me that the feeling doesn't go away even when your kids are seventy.

I was wearing the red suspenders that Jon Bon Jovi had given me for the occasion. People have paid thousands of dollars for my signed suspenders at auctions to benefit charities. Gorbachev and Lady Gaga have shown up in suspenders to meet me. The designer Donna Karan once proposed doing a Larry King line. But it all started as a simple suggestion from an ex-wife of mine after I lost weight following heart surgery:

"Ever wear braces?" Minutes after I wore them on the show, complimentary calls starting coming in. The rest is history . . .

I went to the set early to take pictures with everyone on the staff. The global backdrop has been called one of the ten most recognized images in the world. There were three backdrops: one in Washington, one in New York, and one in Los Angeles. One will be going to The Newseum. Another was cut up into chunks and given to every member of the staff as a memento. The last one stays on for my specials.

I looked at the microphone on my desk. It's not a working mike. It's a prop, but more than a prop. It's a symbol of where I came from. I've always looked at television as radio with a camera. To me, that microphone is a symbol of connection. I was a creature of comfort to millions of people who were up at night during my coast-to-coast radio days. That's the closest tie you can have as a broadcaster. If you were a student or a pilot at that time, you counted on me at night. I did my best to bring that same connection to television. Just being there, saying "Good evening," night after night. After a while, it may not even matter who the guest is. Just that you're there to say "Let's take a call," or "I'll be right back."

I've always said, this ain't brain surgery. But in one small way it is. You feel like you don't ever want to let down the people who've come to see you. I remember Joe DiMaggio being asked why he hustled so much. He said, "The people who were there today may never see me again." I know just what he meant. Whenever I look at that microphone, it reminds me: I owe them my best.

There were many surprises planned for the final show; I went in without knowing who was coming. Well, I knew that Bill Maher and Ryan Seacrest would be with me for the evening. But that was all I knew.

Many people thought I lobbied for Ryan as my replacement. That's not true. I wasn't involved in the process. But I've always said he'd have been a great choice. I don't know if he has the background in politics, but he's dynamic, smart, funny, and comfortable in the chair. On this one night, he had the blue cards in front of him that contained all the surprises and guided the show. So, in a way, he was in charge.

And you've got to hand it to Bill Maher. Right at the top he said he didn't want it to be a funeral—and his humor made sure it wasn't. After Governor Schwarzenegger came on to declare it Larry King Day in California, Bill kicked in with, "The proclamation was stuck in the legislature for two years."

Then came a video clip from President Obama: "You say that all you do is ask questions, but for generations of Americans the answers to those questions have surprised us, they have informed us, and they have opened our eyes to the world beyond our living rooms. So thank you, Larry, and best of luck."

Maher followed that with, "John Boehner is calling and he disagrees completely. He's calling Obama a socialist for those remarks."

Then it was old friends time—though I never think of Regis Philbin as old. He's evergreen to me. Donald Trump appeared, Suze Orman, Dr. Phil. I'd never thought of it before that night, but you don't see too many bald guys on television. Dr. Phil is calm, compassionate, strong—and damn good at what he does. It doesn't matter if you're in real estate, finance, or psychology, you don't stay around this long without being good. There's a lot to be said for longevity.

There was a wacky segment in which Fred Armisen of *Saturday Night Live* came on and impersonated me. Same glasses, same red polka-dotted tie and red suspenders. He was me interviewing me. I'm not sure how well it worked. But there were some laughs, and no show goes perfectly.

Then came the four anchors: Barbara Walters, Brian Williams, Diane Sawyer, and Katie Couric. I had no idea that Katie has been writing poetry for years. She and my producer, Wendy, wrote one that was not only touching, but had some lines that stick with me.

You made NAFTA exciting, and that's hard to do.
And you scored Paris Hilton's post-jail interview.

You went gaga for Gaga, Sharon Stone, Janet Jackson.
Alas, it was Brando who gave you some action.

The next surprise was Bill Clinton via satellite from Arkansas. He looked like he'd totally rebounded after his heart surgery earlier in the year. And just the week before, he'd given a press briefing for Obama at the White House. So I said, "We're both in the Zipper Club. By the way, you looked very good in the briefing room at the White House. Did that make you yearn to return?"

Bill said no. I began to move on. I didn't realize that there were people who didn't understand what I meant by the Zipper Club. Apparently, some people were wondering about another sort of zipper. So Greg, in the control room, came on in my earpiece, as he's done so many times before, to set things straight. When I explained to viewers that I was referring to the zipper scar left by surgery, Bill smiled and said, "I'm glad you clarified that."

That's the thing about Bill Clinton. He's impossible to dislike. Take the person who hates Bill Clinton the most, put him in a room with him, and he'll love him in fifteen seconds.

A camera panned the control room. For seventeen years Wendy Walker has been with me—sometimes calling me more than ten times a day. Cannon was sitting on her lap. She'll remain as close as family.

Then there was a heartfelt moment with Anderson Cooper. Anderson is a very different broadcaster from me. It's amazing how he does it. Not only does he put his life on the line, but he puts his thoughts on the line—like how critical he was of officials during Hurricane Katrina. You always know where he stands. And his words came straight from the heart once again.

He talked about a lunch we'd had recently—a lunch in which we'd spoken about our fathers. Anderson had also lost his father as a child, when he was ten.

He pulled out a letter that his dad had written to him before he died and read from it as the clock ticked down on my final show. It said: "We must go rejoicing in the blessings of this world, chief of which is the mystery, the magic, the majesty, and the miracle that is life." Anderson said I had done just that—and he imagined how proud my father would be.

It's been sixty-eight years since my father died. But I think I know what he would have felt. *Nachas*, it's called in Yiddish. A pride in the happiness that you've helped give someone you care about. I know this feeling. I know it because I felt it a few minutes later. I felt it when my young boys came on the set with Shawn. Chance, the serious one, said he'd be happy to have me at home more. I don't think he knows how I steeled myself so that I didn't cry after my father's death, but he told me it was OK to cry on the show's final night. And then there was Cannon, the comic, who did his impression of me. First the chin in the fist, then the glance at the watch. Then, the gravelly voice: "Where's Shawn? Get in the car! I'm too old for this. I've done this for fifty years!"

That was the highlight of the evening for me. And there was Shawn. It had not been an easy year for her. But there she was, made-up, beautiful, radiant—and looking forward to our future.

Tony Bennett came in right on time. From the middle of a concert, he sang "The Best Is Yet to Come." Then Tony had his audience give me a standing ovation.

The final moments approached. I had no idea what I was going to say at the close, but then I never know what I'm going to say. The only thing I knew was I was not going to use the word *goodbye*. This is what came out:

"I don't know what to say except to you, my audience, thank you. And instead of goodbye, how about so long?"

Then I watched a spotlight shine on the microphone and the entire set fade to black.

We were in a rush to get to the party at Spago. Hundreds of people were waiting. I tried zipping up my jacket, but the zipper wouldn't catch. Cannon said, "Here, Dad, let me do it." And he zipped it up.

Then I was coming down the red carpet and into a swirl of people all wanting to tell me something good. It's hard to explain how that makes you feel. There was my brother, who watched it all from the beginning, and his wife, who helped nurse me through heart surgery; my older kids, Andy, Chaia, and Larry Jr.; the gang from Nate 'n Al's. I was even happy seeing the suits from CNN. Every time I turned, I'd see Kirk Kerkorian or Jane Fonda or Jimmy Kimmel. Jimmy wanted to know if Cannon could come on his show. I was hungry and grabbed a couple of slices of Wolfgang Puck's pizza. It was a great evening, but I have to be honest: I'd much rather have been at a party honoring someone else. With all the toasts and speeches and hugs, you know what I was thinking? *I've got to get the kids home. They've got school tomorrow.*

The next morning I was up at 6:15 a.m.—just like always. As soon as my eyes opened, I shot out of bed, ready to go.

It would take a while, but in time, I understood that the advice Colin Powell had given me about leaving was only half right. When the subway reaches the last stop and is getting ready to go back, it's true that it's time to get off that train. But as Shawn said, "That's when it's time to get on another train."

13

Comedy

If I had a chance to do it all over again . . .

I'd do just what I'm going to do now.

Be a stand-up comic.

There's no more exhilarating feeling than walking out on a stage and making people laugh. It's orgasmic. I've always dreamed of doing a one-man show on Broadway. Who knows? Maybe in the future it'll be one more thing that I can't believe ever happened to me. For now, I'm taking a comedy show on the road. A guy asked me if I'm going to wear suspenders. What did he expect? A cape and a *Phantom of the Opera* mask? I'm not going to reinvent myself. I'm just going to show the world another side of me.

And if there is a touch of sadness left behind by the ending of *Larry King Live*, this is the best way to deal with it. As the playwright Neil Simon once told me, comedy is tragedy turned inside out.

The stories I'll tell in my comedy show will be embellished

a little—but they're all true. They come from the panicky moments and foxholes of my life. Like the time when the Mafia guy who owed me a favor asked me if there was anybody I didn't like. Or the day before open-heart surgery when I met my surgeon for the first time and counted only nine fingers. I would definitely list the day of Moppo's assembly as one of the five worst of my life—right up there with my father's death and Bobby Thomson's home run against the Dodgers. But now that day brings only smiles. Almost everything can become funny over time if you look at it the right way.

If you've ever seen me as a guest on late night shows you'll have a sense of what my comedy show will be like. On *Larry King Live* I asked one-sentence questions. But I'm very different when I'm in the other seat. I once made Jon Stewart fall out of his chair.

My challenge is the one faced by every comic. You're standing on that stage, and there's no telling if the audience will laugh. As Sinatra once said to me, "What if it ain't there? That goes through you for a minute. What if when I walk out, I don't get that prize?"

The good news is, a lot of the material is unbombable. My stories have been refined over decades. Plus, I'm working the show out with my nephew Scott Zeiger, who produced Billy Crystal's *700 Sundays*. A long time ago, I gave Scott his start by getting him a job at Ringling Bros. and Barnum & Bailey Circus. Now he's showing me how to put together a big-time show.

Most important of all, I'm going out there with the passion of a kid getting to live his dream. But I have one big advantage: I'm seventy-seven years old. Inside me, there'll be a piece of all the great comics who have made me laugh since I was a boy.

A little Don Rickles. Some Mel Brooks. And a few others I'd like to nod to simply because they make me smile . . .

Abbott and Costello

"Who's on First?" may be the best comedy skit ever. I never realized that Abbott and Costello's TV show was the model for Jerry Seinfeld's sitcom until my final interview with Jerry.

Bud and Lou always came out in front of the curtain at the beginning of their show. Jerry ended each show doing stand-up in front of a curtain. Bud and Lou lived in an apartment house. They were always running into people and getting into hijinks. Same with Jerry, George, Kramer, and Elaine. All silly, with very little depth, but lots of laughs.

Another thing I didn't realize until my final show with Jerry is that most comedians are left-handed. Jerry passed that on as he signed an autograph. He told me that 60 percent of comedians are lefties, as compared with 9 percent of the total population. It has something to do with the right brain being the center of creativity.

I guess I'm in the minority. I'm a righty, but I'm funny.

Groucho Marx

I would love to have met Groucho. I just barely missed him one morning years ago. He was taking out food from Nate 'n Al's as I came through the door.

All comics want you to love them. They're all pleading: *I'll deprecate myself. I'll do anything.* But, please *laugh.* All comics except Groucho. Groucho was the only great comic who never asked for your sympathy. His comedy was attitudinal. He didn't give a damn.

"I wouldn't want to belong to any club that would accept me as a member."

That's genius. That's when you're above it all.

Don Rickles

It was always the half-truth with Rickles—a safe attack.

He'd see Sinatra in the audience. "Frank . . . Frank . . . The chambermaid, Frank? Couldn't go an hour without it, huh, Frank?"

Joey Bishop would be laughing, and then Rickles would tag it with: "Joey, you can laugh. Frank says it's OK."

So, it's risky. But is it risky? He hits, but not hard enough to hurt anybody. It's over the line. But nobody ever comes back over the line to attack him—although Don tries to make you think retaliation is imminent.

Like the night Sidney Poitier and I were at a table at the Fontainebleau to see him.

Rickles walked onstage and saw us.

"Jeez, Larry, you'll hang around with anybody, huh? Sidney, I don't know what you're doing here. No fried chicken. No watermelon."

Sidney was laughing, but Rickles turned to the band in a panic: "Is he coming up? . . . Is he coming up? . . ."

Mel Brooks

Mel Brooks is the funniest person I've ever met. I've always loved his definition of comedy and tragedy: "Comedy is when you fall down an open manhole. Tragedy is when I cut my finger."

I was one of the first disc jockeys to play his *2,000 Year Old Man* album. You can't tell someone what's funny. But to me, if you don't think the *2,000 Year Old Man* is funny, there is something severely wrong with you.

Carl Reiner asked Mel, in character as the 2,000 Year Old Man, "Did you know Freud?" There are a million things Mel could have done with that. But he went with: "What a basketball player! Best basketball player in Europe!"

"*Basketball?*"

"You don't know about the basketball? Your books don't tell about basketball? Oh, I know why. He passed off. He fed the other guys. He was a point guard. He didn't like to shoot."

So, now, Reiner asks the logical follow-up question: "What about psychiatry?"

As if as an afterthought, Mel says, "That was good."

"How about Shakespeare? Did you know Shakespeare?"

"Of course I knew Shakespeare."

"What a great writer!"

"Hold it! Stop! Whoops! P looked like an R. S looked like an F. Failed penmanship three straight years!"

That's lasting. That doesn't go away. It's like *The Honeymooners*. It holds up. The great ones are never dated.

Comedy is based on the element of surprise. It can also diffuse the tensest of situations. Mel was a master at both because he's so quick. On opening night of *The Producers*, an angry guy from the audience came running over to him at intermission. "I served in World War II," he said. "You are making fun of that war! You're making Hitler into a comic. You are humiliating everyone who served! I've never been so embarrassed. I'm ashamed of this show."

Mel says, "You were in World War II?"

The guy says, "Yeah."

Mel says, "So was I. Where were you? I didn't see ya . . ."

Mel could also set you up. One time, he was booked to fly to Washington for my all-night radio show. "Can you meet me at the airport?" he asked. "I can get a limo, I know, but it'll be nice if you drive out."

So I went out to Dulles. I waited. He walked off the plane with a crowd behind him. As soon as he saw me, he turned to everybody and yelled, "Did I tell ya? When I do a show, the host comes to the airport!"

Lenny Bruce

Every comedian you see now who uses profanity owes Lenny a debt. If there had been no Lenny Bruce, there would have been no Richard Pryor. No Richard Pryor, no Eddie Murphy. No Eddie Murphy, no Chris Rock. Chris Rock gets paid for doing the same thing that Lenny Bruce got arrested for doing.

Lenny was the first one to curse onstage. He changed the culture. But he didn't curse just to curse. There was a point behind it. He used words to make you think.

He'd say: "Fuck is colloquial for intercourse. So, I don't get mad if somebody says 'Fuck you, Lenny!' And if I get mad at someone, I tell him, 'Unfuck you, forever!'"

Although he was infamous at the time for his language, I think he was arrested more for the way he spoke about religion. But it didn't matter how much he got fined or arrested. He refused to change. Bob Hope would go see him and say, "Lenny, lighten it up a little bit and you'll get on every television show in the world." But Lenny wouldn't go on *Ed Sullivan*. It was frustrating. It was easy to want him to be what he refused to be. He was a great mimic. He did a great Chaplin. He just wouldn't cop out. He thought it was insane to be upset over language.

Once while performing in San Francisco, Lenny used the word *cocksucker* onstage. The police hauled him away and drove him to night court.

In the car, the cop driving said, "You're a funny guy. A *real* funny guy. Why do you have to say words like that?"

Lenny says, "It's just a word. Ever had your cock sucked?"

The cop sitting with the driver said, "Ah, the wife don't like it."

The driver said, "Your wife don't like that? It's the best thing."

"Oh, my wife . . . How do I get my wife to do it?"

Now Lenny's giving him advice. He tells him to take a banana to bed.

So all the way down to court they're talking about blow jobs. They get to the court. Reporters have followed them. The court is packed.

Next case: Lenny Bruce.

The charge: Lewd and lascivious language in a public place.

The judge says, "What did he say?"

The cop says, "I'm sorry. I can't repeat it in an open court."

Lenny, of course, was his own best lawyer even though he had an attorney. He says, "Your honor, you can't rule unless he repeats it."

The judge says, "He's right, you've got to repeat it."

The cop says, "I'm embarrassed." So he whispers it: "*Cocksucker.*"

The judge can't hear him. He says, "What?"

The bailiff says, "Cocksucker!"

The judge says, "Cocksucker!"

The whole court erupts, "Cocksucker!"

It's like an opera.

And Lenny says, "I charge this court with lewd and lascivious behavior!"

I think he got acquitted.

Lenny's humor was really about the way he used his intelligence to turn the world upside down so it could be seen clearly. He wasn't generally a joke teller. But this is one that I'll always remember.

The greatest argument in the history of mankind, he said, is between the environmentalists and the geneticists. The geneticists claim you are the way you are because of your genes. The environmentalists contend that you are the way you are because of the way you were raised.

Here's a story that doesn't give any answers, but shows you just how deep the problem is.

A family is in Yellowstone National Park for a weekend. On the way home, they suddenly remember they forgot their six-month-old boy. Now, they've got a choice. If they go back and get the kid, the father will have to miss a sales meeting. There won't be another sales meeting the next day. But, hey, you can always have another kid. So they go home and leave the kid in the park.

The kid is raised by wild dogs. That's all he sees for eighteen years—wild dogs. No humans. Just wild dogs. One day, one of the dogs, in a fit of understanding, drops him on the side of the road and leaves.

The kid is picked up by a hitchhiker and is integrated into society. He enrolls at the University of Chicago. Makes Phi Beta Kappa. The president of the University of Chicago says in the history of the school this is the brightest kid with the most promising future—and then, damnit, one day he's killed chasing a car.

Joan Rivers

What makes somebody funny? That's an impossible question. It reminds me of the greatest answer ever in horse racing. The jockey Willie Shoemaker was asked about one of his competitors: What makes him a great jockey? And he said, "Horses run for him."

Joan Rivers keeps a catalog of every joke she's told. But if she gave you or me that catalog, and we told those jokes, they might not be funny. Joan Rivers is funny because she makes people laugh.

George Carlin

George Carlin became our Lenny—except he didn't get busted.

The most amazing thing to me is how he remembered all his material—it was so involved. He used to do the weatherman, make fun of disc jockeys, the sportscaster. "Here are tonight's scores: 6–3. 2–1. And now, a partial score: 6."

It's not good to say you have a great joke before you tell it, because it's a letdown if people don't laugh. But this is a great joke from Carlin:

A Catholic kid goes into confession. "Forgive me, Father, for I have sinned."

"Yes, son, what did you do?"

"I cannot say."

"You must confess, or I cannot give you absolution."

"Well, Father, I had relations with a young girl."

"I will forgive you. But who was the young girl?"

"Sorry, Father, I cannot betray a confidence."

"It would help a lot to give forgiveness if I knew who the young girl was. Was it Angela Latrice?"

"I cannot say, Father."

"Was it Betty Santangelo?"

"I cannot say."

"OK, you're absolved. But for *four* months you cannot be an altar boy."

The kid comes out of the confessional box and his friend asks, "What happened?"

The kid says, "I got two great leads and I don't have to work for four months."

Henny Youngman

Henny was known for his one-liners. But there's a story my friend George Schlatter loves to tell that shows him off-the-cuff.

Henny invited George to eat at the Carnegie Deli. "Come by for lunch, the family's here. I want you to meet everyone. Just come by to say hello."

So George goes over as the family is finishing up a big lunch. George has a cup of coffee, and the server places the check in front of him.

George picks up the check—and Henny says to make sure to leave a big tip.

George says, "Henny, I can see picking up the check. But the tip, too?"

Henny says, "I don't want you to look cheap."

Milton Berle

Once, Berle and Jack Carter were at a Henny Youngman performance. They let him tell the run-up to one of his jokes, like this:

"A Polish guy buys a zebra for a pet. You know what he calls him?"

And then, before he could say another word, Berle and Carter shouted out the punch line: "Spot!"

David Letterman

David Letterman is one wacky guy. First of all, he keeps the temperature in his studio at about forty-eight degrees. When you go onstage, you're freezing. It warms up a little when the lights are on you. But maybe an undertone of discomfort plays into his humor.

A person could have been on his show forty times, but it wouldn't matter, he'd never say hello beforehand. That's how he works. When you come on, he'll greet you with a big hug, then not say anything to you during the commercial break. One time, during a big intro, as he was hugging me, he whispered in my ear: "I hate my tie."

We did a nice first segment. As soon as we broke, he looked at his tie and said, "Why did I wear this?" He was tortured. "Why did I wear this?"

"You wanna change ties?"

"No, they'll notice. They'll notice."

Then he calls to his producer. "You let me wear this tie!"

But out of nowhere, he'll come up with the perfect line. Like the time I came on a couple of days after a crazy airplane experience. I had been flying across country with the talk show host Cyndy Garvey and some other friends. As we were landing, the winds were so strong that they blew the plane backward. It was unbelievable. The gusts must have flung us five hundred feet in reverse. The pilot recovered and landed us safely, but afterward he told us he'd never experienced anything like it.

I told Letterman the entire story on the air. "What if the plane had crashed?" I said. "Can you imagine what the headline would have been the next day?"

"Yeah," Letterman said. "CYNDY GARVEY AND FIVE OTHERS PERISH."

Jay Leno

Jay is the opposite of Letterman in that he comes by before the show to say hello.

He works very hard. I can remember years ago when he'd call CNN for the overnight news as soon as he got up in the morning so he could get started on his material.

If you ever get a chance, see him in Vegas. His Vegas act is much different from what he does on *The Tonight Show*. He stalks the stage. Three times as much energy.

I guested on his show shortly after *Larry King Live* ended and we did a nice bit.

"I want to ask you something honestly," he said for the cameras. "Do you miss the routine of doing the show after twenty-five years?

"You know something," I told him. "I've got to be honest with you. I never even think about it."

"Never think about it?"

"Never."

The phone rings. I pick it up. "Albuquerque, you're on the air!"

Conan O'Brien

"There's a rumor that NBC is so upset with me they want to keep me off the air for three years. My response to that is if NBC doesn't want people to see me, just leave me on NBC."

Jimmy Kimmel

I don't go on the Internet. But if I did, I'd go to YouTube to see the clip of Jimmy talking to kids in Hollywood while he's dressed up as a chimpanzee.

Jimmy Fallon

Jimmy had Tiger Woods on not long ago. He said, "I want to say thank you for having the courage to come on a late night comedy program. . . . It must have been painful and awful—everything you went through. But from a comedian's standpoint, and my monologue writer's, thank you! . . . Not even making jokes—it kind of wrote itself: Balls, shafts, holes, foursomes . . . Thank you, thank you, thank you!"

When you can make Tiger Woods laugh at what happened to him, you're funny.

Lewis Black

Nobody makes anger funnier.

Woody Allen

"I'm not afraid of death. I just don't want to be there when it happens."

Larry David

What's the expression? A comic says funny things. A comedian sees things funny. Larry David sees things funny.

The situations he puts himself in are amazing. He never really behaves badly—but he's so honest that he gets himself into all sorts of trouble. There's a genius to that.

Larry David is leaving a restaurant. He's got his claim check for the valet. A black guy is standing next to him, and Larry gives him the claim check. The black guy is waiting for *his* car. Larry didn't mean anything wrong by it, but . . .

Bill Maher

Bill used to come on my radio show in Washington back in the eighties when he was just starting out. He'd dissect the political landscape for two hours and take calls. Nobody really knew him. Then look what happened. Last year, I introduced him when he got his star on Hollywood and Vine. When I did, I saw Kato Kaelin in the audience.

"Hey, Kato," I said, "who's house you living behind now?"

"Tiger Woods's," he said.

Bill was the perfect guy to have as a guest the night I announced my resignation. He came on with little notice and no preparation and turned what could have been a difficult night into a lot of laughs.

"I'm glad you're not being fired for your comments about 9/11," he said. "Oh, no, that was me . . ."

Bill is often misunderstood. People say that he hates America. But he loves America. He wants it to be a better place and he believes that the only way to make it a better place is to criticize what's wrong with it. If we can laugh along with him, so much the better.

One night, he went off on Mitt Romney's book, titled *No Apology: The Case for American Greatness*.

"Really?" he said. "Always waving the big foam number one finger. We're not number one in most things. We're number one in military. We're number one in money. We're number one in fat toddlers, meth labs, and people we send to prison.

"We're not number one in literacy, in money spent on education. We're not even number one in social mobility. Social mobility means basically the American Dream, the ability of one generation to do better than the next. We're tenth. That's like Sweden coming tenth in Swedish meatballs."

Stephen Colbert

Colbert is basically doing a parody of Bill O'Reilly. So when I went on his show, I did a parody of Larry King. I parodied his parody. We had fun.

Afterward, he said, "I was going to say it on the air, but I'll tell it off the air: My first sexual experience was in a car, and you were on the radio. I was in college—in the back seat."

211

"Was it romantic?" I asked.

He said, "You had a good guest."

Jackie Gleason

Jackie was very much a perfectionist. There were no satellites in those days. He'd do a show for the East Coast. Later on, they'd play it for the West Coast. In between, he'd watch and know if the third violin was off.

He was not a joke teller; he was a sketch comic. He needed that rotund physique. There was a time when he lost a lot of weight and he wasn't funny.

Before he died, he told me he wanted to do *The Odd Couple*. I said, "Jackie, that's right up your alley. You'd be a great Oscar."

"I don't want to be Oscar," he said. This shows you how Jackie understood comedy. "Oscar's easy. I want to be Felix. You play off Oscar. Oscar has one note. Felix has layers. As Felix you get bigger laughs."

Kathy Griffin

"I have a very unusual stance, which is that I am pro-gay marriage, but I believe that heterosexual marriage should be a criminal offense because I'm divorced and a little bitter."

Craig Ferguson

I can only hope to be as free flowing as Craig when my show gets to the question-and-answer session with the audience.

Craig is from Scotland. I once asked him, "What's under a kilt?"

He didn't miss a beat. "On a good day," he said, "lipstick."

Bob Hope

I can't explain it, but I never thought that Bob Hope was funny.

Colin Powell

Not many people are aware that General Powell has a great sense of humor.

When I was in Washington, the hot invitation in town every New Year's Eve was Ben Bradlee's party. Ben was the managing editor of the *Washington Post* at the time, and anybody who was anybody was at his home on that evening.

The first time I went, the music was playing but nobody was getting up to dance. So Colin and I got up and started dancing together. It became a ritual. For years, we opened up the dance floor by dancing together.

In the fourth year, I said to him, "Think of it. A poor Jewish kid from Brooklyn. A black kid from the South Bronx. Who would've thought that the editor of the *Washington Post* would invite them to a New Year's Eve party and they'd be dancing together."

Colin leaped back and said, *"You're Jewish?"*

Colin has become *mishpocheh*—family. Whenever we see each other he's got a joke in a Yiddish accent.

This is the one Colin told me after the last time I interviewed him.

A Jewish woman says to a friend, "I've got to tell somebody! I've got to admit it! But how do I say it? How do I say it? I can't tell anybody."

"Please tell me," the friend pleads.

"OK. I'm having an affair."

"Who's catering?"

Robin Williams

He's so fast you can't even remember afterward what he said. But you were laughing.

Shecky Greene

"I've got a four-hour erection."

"Call the doctor!"

"I will not!"

Steven Wright

I'm still amazed by creativity. After all these years, I haven't heard it all. I can still hear something new that makes me laugh.

Steven Wright's mind is in another league.

"Doesn't it bother you that *Monopoly* has only one manufacturer?"

Monopoly is a monopoly. What made him think of that?

Mark Russell

Mark is a great political comedian. He plays the piano and relates popular songs to politics. The thing is, we do kind of look alike. One day he was walking through the Atlanta airport and passed three pilots. One said, "Hey, that's Larry King!"

Russell looked over and said, "Fuck you!"

The best part of the joke is that he kept walking. He did it just so he could tell me, "I don't think I did you a favor the other day . . ."

Jon Stewart

"Democrats always seem to have to prove to America that they love America. Republicans love America. They just seem to hate about 50 percent of the people who live in it."

Jon is the Mark Twain of our time. He does the fastest half hour on television. Who else would come on my show after I announced that I would be leaving and say, "What's happening, baby? Can I tell you something? You made the right choice. You are leaving this place. You know what you are? You're the last guy out of a burning building, my friend! . . . Oh, I'm sorry. Am I . . . are we *on* CNN right now?"

George Burns

Even at the end, Burns presided over the Hillcrest Country Club. He made them put up a sign that said it all:

NOBODY UNDER AGE 98 MAY SMOKE

Saturday Night Live

Saturday Night Live is America's weekly campfire. I've seen about 70 percent of them since the days of the original cast.

That show had giants: John Belushi. Chevy Chase. Steve Martin. Bill Murray. I interviewed the show's creator, Lorne Michaels, and some of the show's recent stars last year.

Saturday Night Live has been around for thirty-five years and had a lot of fun with me during that time. It once began a show with a sketch of my wedding to Shawn.

But the bit that always stuck with me is the one about the famous philosopher. It's not all that funny—it's more just true. The philosopher had a new book out about the philosophy of life.

An interviewer asks, "Can you briefly tell us what your philosophy is?"

"Yes. My philosophy is to live in the *now*."

"What does that mean?"

"That means you've got to live in the *now*. Because as soon as it's over, it's a *was*. You can't do anything about the next minute, because it's in front of you. You can't do anything about the minute you just lived. So you've got to live in the *now*. You've got to grab the *now, now*."

You're frantic. Because all you've got is the *now*. And see, this *now*, it's already gone.

So, I'm still going to be waking up at 6:15 every morning. As soon as my eyes open, I'll be shooting out of bed. I'll be trying to make the best of all of my *nows*.

The last words I said on *Larry King Live* were: "Instead of goodbye, how about so long."

But that's not how this book is going to end. This book is going to end with the start of a new chapter. And my new chapter is going to begin like this:

All these years you've been listening to me and watching me, I've been sitting down.

Next time I see you, I'll be standing up.

Index

219

Index

Index